You are a Priest and a Warrior
Copyright © 2016, by Rich I

ISBN 978-0-9972378-1-8 (Paperback)

Library of Congress Control Number: 2016909687

Book cover Family Crest created by Jeff Klena. Crest illustration and book cover design by Dean Estes.

Scripture quotations marked (NIV) are taken from the Holy Bible, New International Version®, NIV®. Copyright © 1973, 1978, 1984, 2011 by Biblica, Inc.™ Used by permission of Zondervan. All rights reserved worldwide. www.zondervan.com The "NIV" and "New International Version" are trademarks registered in the United States Patent and Trademark Office by Biblica, Inc.™

Scripture quotations marked (CJB) are taken from the Complete Jewish Bible by David H. Stern. Copyright © 1998. All rights reserved. Used by permission of Messianic Jewish Publishers, 6120 Day Long Lane, Clarksville, MD 21029. www.messianicjewish.net.

Scripture quotations marked (ESV) are from the ESV® Bible (The Holy Bible, English Standard Version®), copyright © 2001 by Crossway, a publishing ministry of Good News Publishers. Used by permission. All rights reserved."

Scripture quotations marked (MSG) are from THE MESSAGE. Copyright © by Eugene H. Peterson 1993, 1994, 1995, 1996, 2000, 2001, 2002. Used by permission of Tyndale House Publishers, Inc.

Scripture quotations marked (LEB) are from the Lexham English Bible. Copyright 2012 Logos Bible Software. Lexham is a registered trademark of Logos Bible Software. Used by permission.

"Scripture quotations taken from the (NASB) New American Standard Bible®, Copyright © 1960, 1962, 1963, 1968, 1971, 1972, 1973, 1975, 1977, 1995 by The Lockman Foundation Used by permission." www.Lockman.org

On occasion, *italics* or **bold** markings are added to scripture quotations for emphasis.

Excerpts taken from My Utmost for His Highest by Oswald Chambers, © 1935 by Dodd Mead & Co., renewed © 1963 by the Oswald Chambers Publications Assn., Ltd., and is used by permission of Discovery House, Box 3566, Grand Rapids MI 49501. All rights reserved.

Excerpts taken from MERE CHRISTIANITY by CS Lewis © copyright CS Lewis Pte Ltd 1942, 1943, 1944, 1952. And is used by permission from The CS Lewis Company Ltd, 1st Floor Unit 4 Old Generator House, Bourne Valley Road, Poole BH12 1DZ UK.

Excerpts taken from Jesus Among Other Gods by Ravi Zacharias © 2000 Ravi Zacharias. And used by permission of Thomas Nelson. www.thomasnelson.com.

The names have been changed in some stories to respect the privacy of those individuals.

You are a Priest and a Warrior
Published by ZIGGY THE LION, LLC
Boise, Idaho
UNITED STATES OF AMERICA
www.ziggythelion.com

All Rights Reserved. No part of this book may be reproduced or transmitted in any form or by any other means, electronic or mechanical, including photocopying and recording, or by any information storage and retrieval system, without permission in writing from the publisher.

Acknowledgements

To my Eagle and Fat Cat comrades
You finished well. You are priests and warriors.

To my friend Dean
Thank you for your constant encouragement, prayer and help with every aspect of the book.

To my three brothers, Bob, Tim and John
Thank you for giving me the "thumbs up."

**To my daughters and their husbands,
Sarah and Shane; Rachel and John**
Thank you for praying and cheering me on.

To my wife Cindi
Thank you for your love, support and daily prayer. I could not have completed the book without your help.

To my son Jeff
I LOVE YOU!
You are a priest and a warrior.

You are a Priest

You also, like living stones, are being built into a spiritual house to be a holy priesthood, offering spiritual sacrifices acceptable to God through Jesus Christ.
— 1 Peter 2:5 NIV

And a Warrior

No, in all these things we are superconquerors, through the one who has loved us.
— Romans 8:37 CJB

Introduction

A few years ago, I felt a stirring in my spirit to do something uncomfortable — to write a book to my 24-year-old, single son, Jeff. I say uncomfortable because I am not a writer by trade. I am also not seminary trained. However, I wanted Jeff and his future sons, and even their sons, to know who I am (or who I was) and how I became a priest and a warrior.

Sharing meaningful thoughts and personal experiences through writing, I have learned, is difficult. This is a very personal book that is written in first person to Jeff. I did not have you, the unknown reader, in mind when I wrote the book.

But after Jeff read the book and we talked about its content, we both decided that it may also be of interest, and valuable, to others.

The core theme throughout the book is Jeff's identity as a priest and a warrior. He became a priest on the day he decided to follow Jesus as his Lord and his Savior. He became a warrior on the day he was born — just like every other man.

As you will discover, I've used personal and family stories, scripture passages, and supporting material to address my three big questions:

1. Who am I?

2. What am I fighting?

3. How do I win?

Please consider these suggestions on how best to read this book:

- If you are a Christian, as awkward as it may seem, try to read this book as if you are, my son, Jeff, to make it more personal. This perspective will help you tap into my heart —a father writing to his only son.

- If you are considering Christianity and you are already kicking a few religious tires, perhaps this book will be of some use to you. Please note that I am not a professional clergyman, however, you might learn something about Christianity from the inside out. I am just a regular guy who is "in the game" — doing life and following hard after God.

- If you are somewhere in the middle, just dive into the book without any expectations. Maybe you will connect a few dots, fill some gaps in your belief system, and have a few aha moments.

Whether you finish the book or not, I hope and pray that you'll discover who you are, what you're fighting, and how to win — God's way.

Blessings,

Rich Klena

Contents

Introduction	You are a Priest and a Warrior	iv
Chapter 1	I am a Priest	1
Chapter 2	I am a Warrior	17
Chapter 3	Holy Priests See God	28
Chapter 4	Warriors Know Their Enemy	43
Chapter 5	The Power In Priests	59
Chapter 6	Warriors Take Action	71
Chapter 7	Priests Praise God	79
Chapter 8	Warriors Have Courage	92
Chapter 9	Priests Forgive	104
Chapter 10	Warriors Play War Games	118
Chapter 11	Priests Pursue Peace	134
Chapter 12	Warriors Have Faith	144
Appendix	Notes and References	152

Chapter 1

I am a Priest

"Don't look at the camera. Smile. Stop sweating. Act natural," I thought to myself. But like in golf, I was concentrating on too many things.

Then someone yelled, "Roll 'em!" The former news reporter shoved his microphone in my face and began, "Hello Rich. Thanks for the interview, but before we get started, what do you do at your company?"

"Well, I uh ... it's like ... um..."

"Cut!" yelled the reporter.

Turning to my senior executives (who were standing next in line for interview training) he announced, "Hey, when you get asked, 'What do you do?' that question shouldn't be *the stumper*!"

The room got very silent and all eyes were back on me as the reporter sighed and repeated his question.

This time my dry mouth spit out the right answer, "I'm a Product Manager and I support the sales team."

I sweated my way through the rest of the interview.

Although I agree with the reporter (about being able to answer that question), a job title does not fully describe a man. What a man *does,* is not who he *is*.

After 30 years in business and volunteering in men's ministries, I've learned that most men struggle with their identities. One man looks in a mirror and sees a student. Another sees a father. Another sees the reflection of a lonely truck driver. Even mature Christians can be confused with their true identity.

After a few decades, questionable activities began to creep back into the lives of the Christians of the early church. Pressure to conform to their local culture stifled their new, spiritual identities. They forgot who they were *in Christ* and what they were supposed to do. They started to proclaim a different gospel — a gospel where it was okay to look and act like everyone else.

As a result, the Apostle Peter wrote a few encouraging letters to both the Jews and Gentiles in the struggling church, to reinforce their identities and to strengthen their faith.

In 1 Peter 2:5 of the NIV Bible he writes:

> "You also, like living stones, are being built into a spiritual house to be a holy priesthood, offering spiritual sacrifices acceptable to God through Jesus Christ."

I am a Priest

Peter continues in verse nine:

> You are a chosen people; a royal priesthood; a holy nation and God's special possession.

As far as I know, this was the first time the New Testament Christians were referred to as "Priests." Peter completes verse nine by explaining what priests were supposed to do:

> [T]hat you may declare the praises of him who called you out of darkness into his wonderful light.

But how do you do that? Better said, how do *we* declare the praises of the one who called us out of our dark and lonely lives and into His wonderful Kingdom?

Son, that is what this book is about. It is my humble attempt to answer a few of life's big questions, starting with, "Who am I?"

The first three chapters focus on every Christian's identity — first as a priest and then as a warrior. Chapter four describes, "What we are fighting?" (our enemy and his evil plan to destroy us). And the last eight chapters share, "How to win God's way."

As you know, I am not a professional writer. I am not a church pastor, academic scholar or theologian. And I am certainly not the voice of God in your life. The Holy Spirit is the voice of God and He speaks to you in various ways including through His written Word in the Bible. I'm just your dad and I love you. So here are a few suggestions and (hopefully) interesting stories to help you navigate the next season of your life.

I Am A Big Man On Campus

In college, I was a good student athlete and had the world by the tail. But with all of my early success, I was miserable because the thrill of winning didn't last. The endless cycle of winning and emptiness produced a frustrating anger in me. It made me edgy and short-tempered. Hopeless thoughts emerged for the first time in my life.

You have heard the testimonies of those who have hit bottom. But my situation was different; I actually hit bottom when I reached the top. Let me explain.

At 20 years old, I was THAT college football player in the school newspaper every week — a Big Man on Campus; at least that's what they said. However, I didn't feel big at all. To my own amazement, I actually felt empty and lost. Somehow I felt betrayed by God. I thought, "Is this it? Is this why I was born?"

On the football field I knew who I was — I was a linebacker and the other team was definitely the enemy. Everything made sense on the field — I knew *who I was* and *what I was fighting*, and I knew how to win!

But *real life* was different. It didn't make sense. And it certainly wasn't a game.

So I asked God three big questions about *how to win in life*:

- Who am I?
- What am I fighting?

I am a Priest

- How do I win?

My family and friends seemed perfectly happy and generally content with their Catholic faith, but for some reason, I wasn't. So I searched for answers in and outside the Catholic Church. Skipping Mass to visit a few Protestant churches was a pretty big deal. I offended some and confused others, but I needed answers. So after sorting out the style and doctrinal differences, I focused on one historical event that changed the course of history: the death and resurrection of Jesus Christ. Although my Bible knowledge was growing, somehow my faith needed to move from my head to my heart. That's the best way I can describe it.

After a month or two, I finished my "due diligence." The historical evidence was convincing and logical. But logic and reasoning didn't convince me to go "all in" for Jesus.

Strangely, it was the lives of my new, Christian friends that made the difference. They had real joy. They had solid faith. They walked the talk. I saw it with my own eyes and I knew it in my heart. It was true. It was all true.

I made my decision: Jesus Christ was now my Lord *and* my Savior. At last the miserable emptiness inside of me was gone. Jesus filled the hole in my heart with His peace and joy! I made it. I was done!

Well, not quite.

Soon the American way of life began to quickly crowd out my newly discovered happiness. After a while, I started to feel empty again.

Like many Christians, I continued to live in two worlds. I prayed for help, but I prayed *my* way. I prayed for more, but it was more of the wrong things. I wanted things and answers that fit my worldview and supported my lifestyle. I wanted to be *that* Christian — the guy with no problems, a big house, a pretty wife and a great job — the Christian picture of success.

When people looked at me I wanted them to see all of the outward evidence that I was blessed. I wanted an American Gospel where I was Aladdin and Jesus was my genie.

I Am An Idol

The Buffalo Bills sent a scout to my home a few days before the 1982 NFL® draft, in the spring of my senior year in college. Surprised and hopeful, I prayed for *any* chance to be a professional football player.

The excitement soon turned into a three-way competition when scouts from the Seattle Seahawks and the Denver Broncos contacted me the following day. It was fun and nerve-racking. Round after round went by without an offer. Finally, during the 12th round, I signed a "free agent" contract with the Bills and set my sights on Buffalo.

I am a Priest

Two-a-days started in the middle of July in upstate New York. The 24-7 heat and humidity was affecting everyone. So when our linebacker coach yelled at us to line it up for "The Fumble Drill," I automatically thought to myself, "Are you kidding me? I haven't done this stupid drill since high school."

As luck would have it, I lined up right behind an All-Pro linebacker with a Super Bowl victory from another team under his belt. I tried to focus as the coach demonstrated this ridiculous drill like a third-grade teacher. But, just before we began, I mumbled, "Come on…Why are we doing this?"

With that, the veteran linebacker whipped around and blasted, "Hey rook, there's a lot of fumbles in the game — and if we get the ball we can score — and if we score more than the other guys we can win — you got that?"

"Got it," I replied, and kept my mouth shut after that.

Son, here's what I learned from that drill. The older veteran players saw the big picture. They knew how to win as a team on and off the field. I got the part about being a team player *on the field*, but it was the *off the field* part that was a problem. I knew all about THAT party scene, but that wasn't me anymore. I knew if I screwed up and partied my way off the team, regret would haunt me for the rest of my life.

So, I drew a lifestyle-line in the sand and answered their daily invites to party after practice with, "Thanks, but not tonight guys; you go ahead. I need to study my playbook." And from that point on I studied, slept and played my heart out — WITH NO REGRETS — NO MATTER WHAT!

A week later we played the Dallas Cowboys at Texas Stadium. It was a great game and a big pre-season win for us. Even though I was an undrafted rookie, the fans still wanted my autograph. That confused me. I wasn't a big deal, yet they persisted. So after the game I became a team player and signed away. The cameras, flashbulbs and the Hollywood atmosphere fed my ego. I tried to focus on my Christian identity, but I couldn't see clearly that night. Neither could the fans. Truthfully, the fans didn't see the Jesus in me at all. They saw a uniform and an idol, yet Rich Klena, the Christian Athlete, was completely invisible.

That night on the flight back to Buffalo I prayed, "Lord, I can't live in two worlds any more. Help me."

Two days later, I woke up to a loud knock and a familiar voice that said, "Klena, Coach wants to see you." My football career was over.

On the long flight home from Buffalo, I knew God had saved me from a life that I could not handle. Perhaps some could handle it — they could be *both* an uncompromising Christian *and* a fantastic NFL player. But I was a baby Christian on the world's stage ready to take a deep dive into the abyss. I was fighting spiritual powers I didn't understand — a powerful culture that ruled everyone and everything.

I felt like two people at war with each other — the Football Idol verses the Christian Servant. I wanted to be both, but I knew only *one* could win.

I Am A Nobody

Getting cut from the NFL was a very difficult setback, but I trusted God. At least, that is what I told everyone. Truthfully, coming back home was awful. No one knew what to say, or how to act. In one day I had gone from a local celebrity to a local nobody. In fact, it was worse than being a "nobody." My so-called friends were auto-magically unavailable. I felt like a loser with "I GOT CUT" stamped on my forehead. And what about my fiancée, Cindi? What was she thinking? Devastating thoughts ran through my head. "She's not going to marry a nobody-loser like me," I told myself. I was not sure about anything anymore, *except* that I loved her. I didn't want to lose her, so I took a risk and re-proposed to her like this:

"Cindi, right now I'm a nobody. I don't have a job and I don't know what I'm going to do with the rest of my life. But I love you. Still want to get married?"

It was the worst re-proposal on the planet, but it was from my heart. She said, "Yes," again!

I quickly got a job and put a ring on her finger, before she changed her mind.

I Am A Family Man

As I look back, my identity transition was not all that easy during my first 10 years of marriage. I simply traded in my football uniform for a three-piece suit and a stroller. I became a family man working for a Fortune 500 company that valued and promoted family men.

Everyone worked long hours from Monday through Friday back then. However, weekends were special — reserved for family. It was part of the culture and everyone understood the boundaries. Saturdays were for yard work, sports and barbeques. Sunday's were for church.

I was the right age, in the right company and quickly climbed the corporate ladder. Finally, I was "somebody" again. Then my job identity began to slowly take over. I became *Rich Klena, the corporate executive* with a wonderful family, great job, big house and a luxury car in Dallas, Texas.

On the outside, everything looked right, but *I* knew something was wrong. When I looked in the mirror, I could barely see Jesus.

I revisited my big three questions: Who am I? What am I fighting? How do I win? But this time I was too busy to get answers. So I shrugged my shoulders and kept doing life — just like everyone else.

I Am A Big-Shot Executive

The advertising agency called in a panic as I drove home from work one Friday evening, but I was in another world — in my happy place — cruising in my black BMW.

Cool and collected, I chatted away on my cell phone while solving every problem. Then I glanced down at the gas gauge and saw I was low on fuel. I pulled off the freeway to fill her up. I balanced the phone on my shoulder, topped off the tank, finished the call, jumped in the car and headed for home.

I cranked up the stereo and got into the weekend mood. Then something very cool happened, as I crossed over the interstate and through a major intersection, people pointed at my car and smiled. So I smiled back thinking, "Yeah baby, that's what I'm talkin' about!" And then another driver pointed and smiled, and another. It was awesome! Then my mind drifted to wondering what we were having for dinner.

Changing lanes, I glanced at my side-view mirror and Holy Crap, I had a 12-foot gas hose hanging out of my tank!

I pulled off the road and sat in an empty parking lot for a while. Finally I got out of the car to check out the damage. "Wow, it's a miracle — nothing broken," I said to myself. Then I put the hose in the trunk, took a deep breath and headed back to the gas station.

You are a Priest and a Warrior

When I arrived I slowly put on my jacket, straightened my tie and combed my hair. Okay, show time — I opened the trunk, grabbed the nozzle and dragged that Loch Ness Monster into the store. What a sight! Everyone stared at me — especially the pimply-faced cashier.

As I gave him the hose, all I could muster was, "Here."

He cleared his throat and without a smile said, "Thanks." Then I winced out a cheesy smile, looked at everyone — and left.

Son, the moral of this embarrassing story (if there is one) is this: God loves you too much to let you wander away from Him. He will use an unusual event, a prickly conversation or a 12-foot gas hose to steer you back to Him. So put God first in your life. It's your duty and it's God's commandment — the first of Ten Commandments.

Unfortunately, as you can see from these events in my life, I didn't completely understand my duty or the importance of God's first commandment. I became a *big shot executive* with little time for God. It took another decade and a shocking phone call from a relative for me to finally "get it" — that I was chosen to be a priest and to put God first in EVERY aspect of my life.

On Labor Day in 2011, I received a phone call from my cousin Joey in New York. After a little small talk he said, "Richie, I've got some bad news. Cousin Albert died."

Confused I replied, "Who's Cousin Albert?"

I am a Priest

"Richie, you better sit down for this," he said.

Then Joey provided some background to the story. He said that when his mom died a year earlier, Albert and his entire family showed up at the funeral. But nobody knew them.

"Wait a minute," I interrupted. "Mom said everyone died in World War II."

Joey replied. "Well, not exactly. Albert was *the secret cousin* — a secret since 1939."

My mind wandered and then I added, "Wow, what a secret — long lost relatives — I wonder ..."

Joey interrupted, "Richie, that's not all of it. Here's the BIG secret. Albert was Jewish!"

I almost dropped the phone. "What did you say? Did you just say, 'Albert was Jewish'? Wait a second, that means we're Jewish too!"

"Yep. How do you like that?"

Then Joey went on to explain that HIS mom had secretly stayed in touch with Albert all those years!

Son, after the call, I sat alone — I did not know where to put it. Later that evening, when I told your mom the story, she said, "Honey, your mom is gone, your aunt is gone, they're all gone. But God wouldn't let it die."

Over the next two years, I searched for answers and a way to understand my new identity. Since the Bible describes the Nation of Israel as a chosen people and God's special possession, I concluded that I must be a super messianic Christian or something like that. And that is when the Holy Spirit completely busted me.

Jeff, at first, I didn't see my self-righteous sin; it kind of snuck up on me. I'm ashamed to admit that deep-down inside I actually thought I *was* something special — more blessed or better than regular Christians. Pretty awful, isn't it?

God used *that* phone call to shake me up — to finally realize that I was already chosen, already special, and already a priest and a warrior in the Kingdom of God. And the Good News of the Gospel WAS and IS a very big deal! I cannot believe it took me 30 years to finally get it. Through Jesus, I am part of God's royal priesthood. Jesus chose me — and I'm special to Him!

Christians Are A Royal Priesthood

John Owen, the great British theologian, in his book, The Holy Spirit[1], referred to Revelation 1:6 when he wrote:

> [T]hey are said to be made kings and priests, or a royal priesthood; for they partake of the same Spirit wherewith he was anointed.

Then, Peter describes *all Christians* this way:

I am a Priest

> You also, like living stones, are being built into a spiritual house to be a holy priesthood, offering spiritual sacrifices acceptable to God through Jesus Christ (1 Peter 2:5 NIV).

> You are a chosen people; a royal priesthood; a holy nation and God's special possession (1 Peter 2:9 NIV).

And the Apostle Paul settles the "chosen" argument with these three scriptures:

> There is neither Jew nor Gentile, neither slave nor free, nor is there male and female, — for you are all one in Christ Jesus (Galatians 3:28 NIV).

> This righteousness is given through faith in Jesus Christ to all who believe. There is no difference between Jew and Gentile (Romans 3:22 NIV).

> For there is no difference between Jew and Gentile, the same Lord is Lord of all and richly blesses all who call on him (Romans 10:12 NIV).

Son, always remember that you are a priest and a warrior. Your "priest identity" is your lifetime constant. Again, your priest identity is your lifetime constant.

As you change professions, get married and start a family, always remember who you are. When faced with ethical decisions on and off the field, remember you are a priest — then make the right choice.

You are a Priest and a Warrior

Demonstrate Christ's love in all of your relationships and then follow the Holy Spirit wherever He takes you.

Chapter 2

I am a Warrior

> In all these things we are superconquerors, through the one who has loved us (Romans 8:37 CJB).

I have no idea what got into me *that* Saturday morning. It started out just fine. We had donuts and coffee just like all the other days before a game. I played in left field, or "Homerun Alley," as we called it. To no one's surprise, our softball team (of former high school football players) had an aggressive personality — nineteen year olds with something to prove.

Towards the end of the game a batter smashed a ball right over my head and into the right field of another game. "Dang it! I knew I should've played deeper!" I thought. "If we lose this game, I'll get ragged on for years."

I caught up to the ball as it rolled to a stop about a foot behind the other game's right fielder. He glanced down at the ball and then up at me, but did not budge — and THAT lit my fuse! So I pushed him aside, grabbed the ball and hit my cut-off guy. Then he pushed me back and added, "Hey, what the f%*&!"

Son, that was all it took!

I spun around and started a pretty nasty slugfest right in front of everyone. Astonished, my friends ran over and pulled me off the guy and said, "Klena, what are you doing?" I did not say a thing. I just walked away. There was no way to explain my behavior, except for the fact that I actually proved something. I proved that I was definitely broken!

I Am Broken

The Merriam-Webster Dictionary defines a warrior as: *a person who fights in battles and is known for having courage and skill.* Warriors stand for something meaningful. They fight with courage and honor. They battle through every obstacle and overcome tremendous adversity. They are born to fight — men with grit who never quit.

Regardless of religion, occupation, size, race or personality, I believe that God created every man as a warrior — a fighter with the will to win. Vince Lombardi once said, *"Winning isn't everything, it's the only thing."* I agree. But the question I had to ask myself was what am I fighting to win? What am I competing for?

Son, before I knew Christ, I was a boxer without a match. I was an independent warrior fighting for an elusive prize conceived in my mind, and pursued by my body. I craved fame, fortune, and power like food and oxygen. I fought all the time, yet I did not really know why.

I am a Warrior

Was I a random freak of nature? No, I was not a freak. I was just broken — a broken warrior in a broken world.

God Is In The Restoration Business

Son, you have heard me say that, "God is in the restoration business." He began with Adam and He continued with the life-giving Spirit of the Messiah. Here is how the Apostle Paul described it:

> "If there is a natural body, there is also a spiritual body. Thus it is written, "The first man Adam became a living being; the last Adam became a life-giving spirit" (1 Corinthians 15:44-45 ESV).

In the first century church, the Apostle Paul was a remarkable living testimony of God's love and restoration power. In my opinion, Paul's conversion is the greatest 180-degree turnaround in history.

A few days after Paul was knocked off his horse, he received the Holy Spirit and immediately told everyone some really Good News about a different way (or The Way) to heaven through Jesus Christ, his new Messiah. Yet some did not see this as good news, so over the next 25 years, Paul was threatened, beaten and almost killed for sharing the Good News about Jesus the Messiah.

Around A.D. 59, Paul decided to go "all in" by telling his amazing testimony to a very hostile crowd consisting of King

Agrippa II (the Great Grandson of Herod), Porcius Festus (the new Governor of Judea), and to many Jewish leaders that wanted Paul dead. Historians believe that this event, recorded in Acts 26, took place near Herod's palace in the beautiful, seaport city of Caesarea.

Jeff, picture yourself in the crowd near this magnificent palace with palm trees and a view of the Mediterranean Sea in the background, as the Apostle Paul (a prisoner still in chains) begins his testimony:

> "The Jewish people all know the way I have lived ever since I was a child, from the beginning of my life in my own country, and also in Jerusalem. They have known me for a long time and can testify, if they are willing, that I conformed to the strictest sect of our religion, living as a Pharisee. And now it is because of my hope in what God has promised our ancestors that I am on trial today.
>
> "This is the promise our twelve tribes are hoping to see fulfilled as they earnestly serve God day and night. King Agrippa, it is because of this hope that these Jews are accusing me. Why should any of you consider it incredible that God raises the dead?
>
> "I too was convinced that I ought to do all that was possible to oppose the name of Jesus of Nazareth. And that is just what I did in Jerusalem. On the authority of

the chief priests I put many of the Lord's people in prison, and when they were put to death, I cast my vote against them.

"Many a time I went from one synagogue to another to have them punished, and I tried to force them to blaspheme. I was so obsessed with persecuting them that I even hunted them down in foreign cities.

"On one of these journeys, I was going to Damascus with the authority and commission of the chief priests. About noon, King Agrippa, as I was on the road, I saw a light from heaven, brighter than the sun, blazing around me and my companions. We all fell to the ground, and I heard a voice saying to me in Aramaic, 'Saul, Saul, why do you persecute me? It is hard for you to kick against the goads.'

"Then I asked, 'Who are you, Lord?'

" 'I am Jesus, whom you are persecuting,' the Lord replied. 'Now get up and stand on your feet. I have appeared to you to appoint you as a servant and as a witness of what you have seen and will see of me. I will rescue you from your own people and from the Gentiles. I am sending you to them to open their eyes and turn them from darkness to light, and from the power of Satan to God, so that they may receive forgiveness of sins and a place among those who are sanctified by faith in me.'

"So then, King Agrippa, I was not disobedient to the vision from heaven. First to those in Damascus, then to those in Jerusalem and in all of Judea, and then to the Gentiles, I preached that they should repent and turn to God and demonstrate their repentance by their deeds."

...Then Agrippa said to Paul, "Do you think that in such a short time you can persuade me to be a Christian?"

Paul replied, "Short time or long — I pray to God that not only you but all who are listening to me today may become what I am, except for these chains" (Acts 26:4-20, 28-29 NIV).

Paul ended his testimony with a prayer that Agrippa and every witness in attendance "may become what I am." Later Paul defined himself as "Called to be an apostle and set apart for the gospel of God" (Romans 1:1 NIV).

Fixed By Jesus

Although there is so much to say about Paul's testimony in Acts 26, I would like to focus on verse 14 for a moment. Let us look at it again:

> "Saul, Saul why do you persecute me? It is hard for you to kick against the goads."

I am a Warrior

Most Christians are familiar with Paul's dramatic conversion on the road to the foreign city of Damascus. The statement, "Saul, Saul, why do you persecute me" is well known. But what about the second part of the statement: "It is hard for you to kick against the goads." Do you know its meaning?

A goad was a thick wooden stick with a sharp point on one end. It was used by farmers to poke an ox in the backside if it resisted pulling a plow or a heavy cart. Goads were very effective tools to show the ox "who's in charge." On occasion, a very stubborn ox resisted its master's prodding with a swift kick, back against the goad, thus inflicting great pain and injury to itself.

Back then everyone knew the meaning of this metaphor. Therefore, it is safe to assume that Christ had been nudging and prodding Paul for some time. Not only had Paul resisted God's prodding, but he aggressively "kicked back" against him. He started a war that injured himself. He started a war he could not win — a war against his countrymen, a war against himself, and a war against the very God that he worshipped and adored.

Void of Christ, there is a lot of Saul in all of us — angry, fighting warriors — broken, proud, hard and stubborn, tearing ourselves apart with every kick against the goads of God. If you think about it, it *was* hard for Paul to kick against the goads. It is hard for everyone — everyone who kicks against God's nudging and prodding to live differently — to live for God, not against him.

Therefore, pray for those you know who are as stubborn as an ox. Like Jesus had compassion for Paul, likewise have compassion for a friend, even if he is at war with everyone and everything. Pray that he stops "kicking against the goads" and ends his war with Jesus.

> It is written: "Come to me, all you who are weary and burdened, and I will give you rest. Take my yoke upon you and learn from me, for I am gentle and humble in heart, and you will find rest for your souls. For my yoke is easy and my burden is light" (Matthew 11:28-30 NIV).

Be A Priest And A Warrior

Jesus has the ability and the authority to fix every broken warrior. Like two magnets, the priest bonds to the warrior. It is a powerful bond when properly aligned with God's will. Positive to negative. Priest to warrior. Spirit to body.

Jesus has the authority to give you supernatural power to advance the Kingdom of God, however, you will not receive His power unless you have been properly aligned with His will. And God's alignment is more like a complete overhaul of your mind. It is a lifetime process that is filled with faith, joy and excitement — and opposition from the enemy of God.

Son, the cunning devil directs the activities of this world like a master puppeteer. His plan is to *separate* you from God, any way that he can. He uses real disasters to accomplish this goal. If you are married, he will try to break your vow of love. If you are wealthy, he will try to bankrupt you. If you are healthy, he may try to make you sick. He will try to steal your joy and rob your hope — his relentless attempt to resurrect your old way of life — to bring back the empty, angry warrior.

All of his strategies fall under one personal mission: to get you to renounce God! If Satan succeeds, then your existence will become meaningless.

But God gave us His powerful Holy Spirit to guide and protect us — to transform us into superconquerors with a new way of living — with a new way of loving that brings honor to God. He also equips us with weapons that are highly effective when properly used. These spiritual weapons cannot be seen in a physical sense, but they work, and can defeat the enemy's evil plans.

You are a priest and a warrior, so use God's weapons like love, forgiveness, patience and integrity to extinguish the flames of injustice, deceit and fear before they ignite a fire that burns up every relationship. As you read each chapter of this book, remember who you are — your identity as a priest *and* a warrior. Learn how to overcome the strategies and tactics of the enemy, and learn how to win God's way.

Be A Superconqueror

You may be a priest and a warrior, but you are not a superconqueror until you receive God's power — and you need God's powerful Holy Spirit to win. That power is released in and through you as the Holy Spirit aligns your plans with God's will. And what is God's will? — to love God by sharing the Good News; to love God by putting Him FIRST in your life; to love God every time you love your neighbor as yourself.

I like the Complete Jewish Bible (CJB) translation of Romans 8:35-39. In the passage below, Paul shows us the fine print of Christianity *and* the hope of our salvation. He does not say as Christians, we are members of the healthy, wealthy, happy, holy club. He does not say that with Christ all of our problems vanish. On the contrary, Paul says *with Jesus* no matter what we encounter — no matter what we experience — we are superconquerors who win!

Here is Romans 8:35-39 CJB:

> Who will separate us from the love of the Messiah? Trouble? Hardship? Persecution? Hunger? Poverty? Danger? War? As the Tanakh puts it, "For your sake we are being put to death all day long, we are considered sheep to be slaughtered." No, in all these things we are superconquerors, through the one who has loved us.

I am a Warrior

> For I am convinced that neither death nor life, neither angels nor other heavenly rulers, neither what exists nor what is coming, neither powers above nor powers below, nor any other created thing will be able to separate us from the love of God which comes to us through the Messiah - Yeshua, our Lord.

Son, Jesus broke the Old Testament's curse with His death and resurrection. That is really Good News. When it was finished, He received authority over everything[2]. Jesus restored the Spirit of God as it was in the days of Adam and created a new kingdom — an everlasting kingdom of *holy priests and warriors* — superconquerors, who love one another and FAITHFULLY serve their Lord and Savior, Jesus Christ.

Chapter 3

Holy Priests See God

> Strive for peace with everyone, and for the holiness without which no one will see the Lord (Hebrews 12:14 ESV).

Holiness is a difficult subject to teach without sounding self-righteous. In fact, discussing holiness with anyone is not very popular. Nevertheless, it is an important aspect of your priest and warrior identity and a pillar of your faith.

So what is holiness? Is it keeping a set of rules? Is it living without sin or being perfect? Does holiness lead to seeing God? If so, how do you get it?

For thousands of years, religions around the world have tried to define holiness within their statements of faith or written doctrines. Although their definitions seem to vary, they do agree on one critical point: *holiness matters*. So they create methods to get holy — or to get holy enough — to win the prize of eternal life.

Typically, it is a list of rules or deeds accompanied by strict performance criteria. The religious doctrine has a specific theme, tone or philosophical opinion that reflects the author's beliefs, who claims to have some sort of secret knowledge that leads to immortality.

These religious authors are nothing more than broken men who fight for significance and a tonic for their pain. It is a complicated matter that requires an "all in" decision by the prospect. So many avoid the subject and punt the topic away. You will recognize these punts in the form of questions like: "Jeff, it doesn't really matter since all roads lead to heaven." But as you know, it *does* matter, and all roads *do not* lead to heaven.

Ravi Zacharias is a well-known author and highly respected speaker. He has defended Christianity and explained its a gracious gift of salvation to seekers and skeptics all over the world. Here is an excerpt from his book, *Jesus Among Other Gods*[3]:

> "You hear it a thousand times and more growing up in the East, 'We all come through different routes and end up in the same place.' But I say to you, God is not a place or an experience or a feeling.
>
> "Pluralistic cultures are beguiled by the cosmetically courteous idea that sincerity or privilege of birth is all that counts and that truth is subject of the beholder. In no other discipline of life can one be so naïve as to

claim inherited belief or insistent belief as the sole determiner of truth.

"Why, then, do we make the catastrophic error of thinking that all religions are right and that it does not matter whether the claims they make are objectively true?

"All religions are not the same. All religions do not point to God. All religions do not say that all religions are the same. At the heart of every religion is an uncompromising commitment to a particular way of defining who God is or is not and accordingly, of defining life's purpose.

"Anyone who claims that all religions are the same betrays not only an ignorance of all religions but also a caricatured view of even the best-known ones. Every religion at its core is exclusive."

Son, although Christianity is exclusive, anyone who hears the call of Jesus and serves Him as Lord and Savior can become a Christian and receive the gift of eternal life. That is the Good News of the Gospel and the common theme in every New Testament epistle.

You can trust the Bible. It is historically credible. It was inspired by one God and written by 40 authors over a period of 1,500 years. All of the inspired authors agreed on one thing: sin separates everyone from God.

Stated differently, the *Good News of the Gospel* is this: Jesus is the gift that removes your sin and your separation from God. He restores us to God so that we can see Him now and for all eternity.

Holiness Is The Gift Of Salvation

Son, here is our lead chapter verse again:

> Strive for peace with everyone, and for the holiness without which no one will see the Lord (Hebrews 12:14 ESV).

Once you receive the gift of salvation or "the holiness," you are set apart to do the "will of God." Let me say that again, Once you receive the gift of salvation or "the holiness," you are set apart to do the "will of God." And just to be clear, you become holy and saved on the day you accept Jesus as your Lord and Savior. It is the epitome of God's grace. God Himself washes you from head to toe and makes you pure and clean.

Jeff, this is the method or "The Way" to eternal life and the only way to *see* God. However, you still live in a dirty and messy world. So how do you stay clean?

On the evening of the Passover Feast, the Apostle John documents a famous story commonly known as "Jesus Washes the Disciples' Feet." This story is the best example that I can find in the Bible of how to remain holy throughout your life.

> It was just before the Passover Festival. Jesus knew that the hour had come for him to leave this world and go to the Father. Having loved his own who were in the world, he loved them to the end.
>
> The evening meal was in progress, and the devil had already prompted Judas, the son of Simon Iscariot, to betray Jesus. Jesus knew that the Father had put all things under his power, and that he had come from God and was returning to God; so he got up from the meal, took off his outer clothing, and wrapped a towel around his waist. After that, he poured water into a basin and began to wash his disciples' feet, drying them with the towel that was wrapped around him.
>
> He came to Simon Peter, who said to him, "Lord, are you going to wash my feet?"
>
> Jesus replied, "You do not realize now what I am doing, but later you will understand."
>
> "No," said Peter, "you shall never wash my feet."
>
> Jesus answered, "Unless I wash you, you have no part with me."
>
> "Then, Lord," Simon Peter replied, "not just my feet but my hands and my head as well!"

Holy Priests See God

Jesus answered, "Those who have had a bath need only to wash their feet; their whole body is clean. And you are clean, though not every one of you."

For he knew who was going to betray him, and that was why he said not every one was clean.

When he had finished washing their feet, he put on his clothes and returned to his place. "Do you understand what I have done for you?" he asked them. "You call me 'Teacher' and 'Lord,' and rightly so, for that is what I am.

Now that I, your Lord and Teacher, have washed your feet, you also should wash one another's feet. I have set you an example that you should do as I have done for you.

Very truly I tell you, no servant is greater than his master, nor is a messenger greater than the one who sent him.

Now that you know these things, you will be blessed if you do them (John 13:1-17 NIV).

Now You Know

This was a *loving* but direct command from our Savior, Lord and *Teacher*. But what specifically did they "now know"? And what exactly were they supposed to do?

You are a Priest and a Warrior

First, RECEIVE GOD'S LOVE. Allow God to love you as a father loves a son — as I have loved you. Be open to coaching and counseling from the Holy Spirit and let Him keep you clean. Trust me son, this is the easy way, because *if you choose to hide your dirty feet, God will bring a few folks into your circle for, what I call, "discussion time."*

This one hurts — Especially if the "folks" are immediate family. It feels like they are pulling you through a car wash by your toes. I know. I have been washed like this a few times.

Secondly, LOVE GOD'S PEOPLE and keep-your-cool if someone approaches you. Remember God directs them as He directs you.

Let the Holy Spirit convict you. If He does, then get clean, or come clean and face the truth and repent. All of this is necessary. It is a commandment from Jesus. A new way of life for those who are in Christ. After your feet have been washed in this matter. Then it is your turn.

But like Peter, a Christian brother may initially refuse to receive your help. You have heard the saying, "Love is blind." I agree. But that example does not apply here. It is not your friend's love that is blind; rather it is his self-righteous behavior that is blind.

You clearly see the blind-spot or that he is blind to the spot — the spot being his pattern of un-Christian behavior — and yet, he continues to dodge your attempts to get together and talk.

If this continues, and his behavior gets worse, then his feet will reek *and* his Christian testimony will stink!

Finally know this: The foot-washing business is messy. It is embarrassing. It is inconvenient. And it is humiliating. But it is the recommended method for giving and receiving Christ's love.

Son, mature Christians get this! So they stay clean and *in love*, and with great humility, they help *others* stay clean.

> As it is written, "How beautiful are the feet of those who preach the good news!" (Romans 10:15 ESV).

Mature Christians Share God's Love

Unfortunately, some Christians are stuck in elementary school with immature thinking and selfish behavior. They want the grace and forgiveness. They want salvation and eternity in heaven, but they do not want to obey and serve Jesus as their Lord, their Savior *and* their Teacher. Hebrews 6:1 of the ESV Bible states:

> Therefore let us leave the elementary doctrine of Christ and go on to maturity.

Son, if you encounter an Elementary School Christian, pray for him. Pray that he will grow up and mature in Christ. Perhaps God will ask you to have a chat with him — to humbly wash his spiritual feet.

You are a Priest and a Warrior

In my opinion, no Christian can ignore God's sanctifying foot-washing process without dire consequences. However, if he succeeds, and continues to willfully sin, then he removes holiness from The Gospel and takes a different road — on the highway to nowhere.

Son, I do not want you to think that holiness means perfection or that I am putting an impossible guilt trip on you. That is not it either. As long as we live on earth, we will sin. But when we do, we must listen to the Holy Spirit and humbly repent and get back on track — back on the right road.

Oswald Chambers was a British missionary, Bible scholar and teacher. After his death about 100 years ago, his wife grouped his sermons into a book called, *My Utmost for His Highest*.

Each daily reading is packed with truth, love and a challenging message that equipped his young missionary students for service around the world. Chambers taught his students well. He taught about truth and tackled every subject, including this section taken from August 15th:

> Whosoever is born of God — does not commit sin (1 John 3:9).

Do I seek to stop sinning or have I stopped sinning? To be born of God means that I have the supernatural power of God to stop sinning. In the Bible it is never should a Christian sin? The Bible puts it emphatically; a Christian must not sin. The effective working of the new birth life in us is that we do not commit sin — not merely that we have the power <u>not</u> to sin, but that we have stopped sinning. First John 3:9 does not mean that we cannot sin; it means that if we obey the life of God in us, we need not sin[4].

Son, now let me dig a little deeper. When we receive God's forgiveness, we must leave that sin behind. If we ignore the Holy Spirit and continue to willfully sin, then we will get used to a particular sin or nasty habit. If this happens, then we will want to change the Gospel to fit our new lifestyle where sin is ok ... whatever "it" is. Can you see how Satan can weasel his way into our minds with false thinking and distorted proclamations of the truth? Our job is to listen and to obey the Holy Spirit and allow Him to do a magnificent, sanctifying work in us as He moves us on to maturity.

Holiness Is A Gift And A Process

The word "sanctification" is not used in our everyday conversations anymore. However, it is used in the Bible to describe the process of how the Holy Spirit continually guides and changes our behavior to make us look more like Jesus. This is how it is accomplished:

When we quiet ourselves in prayer, He speaks to our renewed mind — to help us think and act like differently — to make us more like Him. The Holy Spirit also uses circumstances, Bible verses, spouses, friends and family to get our attention and move us on to maturity — so that he can trust us — so that he can use us!

When I was 27, I became the token "young-guy" board member of a small church in southern California. After a few months, the Senior Pastor invited the entire church to a special, Sunday night service dedicated to prayer. He also asked the elders and board members to make an extra effort to attend and help with prayer after the service.

When I arrived at the church that evening, three of the senior elders asked me if I had ever prayed for anyone before. I said, "Well, what do you mean?" — that was the wrong answer! Then one of them asked, "Has anyone ever laid hands on you before?" I replied, "Laid hands on me?" Now I was 0 for 2.

They explained how prayer actually worked — how God's power flowed through His servants — and that if I loved God and loved His people, then His power would move through me. It all made sense. So they laid their hands on my shoulders and, among other things, prayed for the power of the Holy Spirit to come upon me, to equip me with love and knowledge to pray for others.

At the end of the service, the pastor encouraged those who needed prayer to come forward. Then one of the elders waved me up front. "Okay, here we go," I thought.

But I was totally unprepared for God's next step.

I stood tall and waited for the crowd to come. The others had about 10 people in their lines. I had one.

When I began to pray for that guy, the Holy Spirit revealed, in my mind, specific information about him that was only relevant to his prayer request. It happened again and again. These revelations allowed me to pray more specifically and effectively for careers, health, faith and close relationships.

God answered their prayers that night and it was amazing — and He did it *through me*! I could not explain it, but it was real. The people I prayed for felt God's love as His power flowed through me; and it made my knees weak. I experienced the power of God that night. He chose me to be His vessel-of-love to His hurting people. Yes, I was frightened, but I believed in God, so I stepped out in faith.

For the first time in my life, I knew I was walking on holy ground and doing the work of the Lord. After that night, I was never the same. I understood the elementary concepts of Christianity and moved on to maturity by using His gifts to serve and love others. I experienced the power of the Holy Spirit from our Almighty Creator. I knew deep down in my soul that God existed and that he moved through me — with His power from outside this world — the same power that raised Jesus from the dead.

This event strengthened my faith. The power was real and I could not explain it. It was the catalyst I needed to grow-up and mature — to be used by God whenever He calls. A life where holiness, maturity and effectiveness are tied together in Christian service.

Holy Priests See God

In Peter's second letter to the church, he builds a strong case for our proper understanding of the entire gospel. He also warns against being influenced by false teachers who have a message of, "sin is ok." Although I included the first twelve verses of the letter, when you get time, please read the entire, three-chapter letter, all the way through in one sitting, as if Peter is writing directly to *you*. Peter concludes the letter by describing how holy priests stay on the right path — the path to see God.

> Simon Peter, a servant and apostle of Jesus Christ, To those who through the righteousness of our God and Savior Jesus Christ have received a faith as precious as ours: Grace and peace be yours in abundance through the knowledge of God and of Jesus our Lord. His divine power has given us everything we need for a godly life through our knowledge of him who called us by his own glory and goodness. Through these he has given us his very great and precious promises, so that through them you may participate in the divine nature, having escaped the corruption in the world caused by evil desires.
>
> For this very reason, make every effort to add to your faith goodness; and to goodness, knowledge; and to

> knowledge, self-control; and to self-control, perseverance; and to perseverance, godliness; and to godliness, mutual affection; and to mutual affection, love. For if you possess these qualities in increasing measure, they will keep you from being ineffective and unproductive in your knowledge of our Lord Jesus Christ. But whoever does not have them is nearsighted and blind, forgetting that they have been cleansed from their past sins.
>
> Therefore, my brothers and sisters, make every effort to confirm your calling and election. For if you do these things, you will never stumble, and you will receive a rich welcome into the eternal kingdom of our Lord and Savior Jesus Christ.
>
> So I will always remind you of these things, even though you know them and are firmly established in the truth you now have (2 Peter 1:1-12 NIV).

Peter finished this letter by stressing the importance of holiness, specifically that "Christians should lead holy and Godly lives."[5] In fact, Peter, Paul, James and John all reinforced the importance of "holiness" and warned against false teachers who lie and manipulate the truth.

But you already know this — you are a mature Christ follower who is also in the foot-washing business. Continue on this path, son. Allow the Holy Spirit to help you, as you help others. Remember Romans 10:15:

> How beautiful are the feet of those who preach the good news of the gospel!

Chapter 4

Warriors Know Their Enemy

The Apostle Paul answered my second big question, "What am I fighting?" when he writes:

> For we are not struggling against human beings, but against the rulers, authorities and cosmic powers governing this darkness, against the spiritual forces of evil in the heavenly realm (Ephesians 6:12 CJB).

In this realm, we are fighting something very different — a system of invisible rulers with special powers. Therefore, if you want to win God's way, you must study the Bible in order to recognize the powerful strategies and tactics of the enemy. Otherwise, you will suspect that your family, your friends, your boss, your government or even *your God* are your enemies!

Paul says we struggle "against the rulers and authorities." Son, this simple phrase introduces the structure of this evil kingdom. I imagine it is a military structure with different brigades named jealousy, deceit, pride, destruction, cancer, adultery, greed, power, murder, mockery, gluttony, laziness, hopelessness, doubt and so on. The demonic soldiers in these brigades study us. They learn our patterns and uncover our weaknesses. Then they wait for the right moment to attack — both Christians and non-Christians, alike.

Paul experienced Satan's complete mind-controlling power from two perspectives — first as the persecuting Pharisee, and later as a persecuted saint. With these vivid memories etched into his consciousness, he scripted a loving letter to the Ephesians that ended with detailed instructions on how to defeat Satan and his army of demons.

Let us return to Ephesians 6:12 for a moment where Paul created a new title for Satan — a carefully crafted word that is used only once in the entire Bible. He calls Satan *kosmokratoraV*[6]. It is composed of two Greek words — *kosmos (world)*; and *kratoraV (to take hold of, to seize control)*. Although, *"Ruler of Darkness"* is a common translation for this word, Satan the *"World-controller"* seems more accurate to me. Now think about Satan "The World-controller" as you read this next story about Opa — your Jewish, great grandfather.

Opa was 24-years-old when World War I began. I wish I knew more about him during those years, but no one ever talked about it. I can only speculate that Opa witnessed real evil from the sidelines from 1914-1918, since Holland remained neutral throughout the first Great War.

Warriors Know Their Enemy

Opa was an educated businessman and the owner of an international bookbinding company with offices in Holland and New York. His profession certainly offered him a unique opportunity to objectively evaluate the rapid ascent of the Nazi war machine after WWI.

Over the next two decades, Opa traveled throughout Europe and the United States. He read British, Dutch and American newspapers. He entertained clients and discussed world events with fellow passengers as he sailed back and forth across the Atlantic. He observed Hitler's political rise to power. But more importantly, he observed the cultural and moral shift of an entire continent.

Opa watched and learned. After WWI, the defeated Germans wanted a better life — a Fatherland flowing with milk and honey. Throughout the 1930s, the Nazi-controlled lawmakers slowly and methodically removed the legal rights and seized the personal property of their own Jewish/German citizens. And when they finished stealing from their own countrymen, they fought for more.

C.S. Lewis spoke about man's attempt to "be like gods" during his WWII radio broadcasts. After the war, these broadcasts were assembled into a book called, *Mere Christianity*. In the chapter titled, *What Christians Believe*, Lewis wrote:

> What Satan put into the heads of our remote ancestors was the idea that they could "be like gods" — could set

> up on their own as if they had created themselves — be their own masters — invent some sort of happiness for themselves outside God, apart from God.
>
> And out of that hopeless attempt has come nearly all that we call human history — money, poverty, ambition, war, prostitution, classes, empires, slavery — the long terrible story of man trying to find something other than God which will make him happy.[7]

Radios and newspapers reported Hitler's bold moves as he annexed nations and seized personal property. In March of 1938, he invaded Austria and removed all the rights of the Austrian Jews with a similar pattern of intimidation and force that he imposed upon those who lived in Germany. By September, Hitler annexed a portion of Czechoslovakia, and in March of the following year (1939), he took the rest of it. Again, Opa studied his enemy and as you will read in Chapter 6 of this book, Opa prepared his mind and he took *action*.

The Battle For Your Mind

The battle for your mind is intense. Even as I am writing this chapter, I am tempted to throw this entire book in the trash can. I keep thinking, "I've got to be out of my mind for writing this stuff!" So I pray, and then press on when the Holy Spirit shows me that I am actually *in my right mind* (or Christ's good mind) to write this book to you. Let me switch gears for a moment to further develop the topic of *the good mind of Christ*.

Warriors Know Their Enemy

The Apostle Paul wrote many letters to the leaders of the early church. As you would expect, the themes or topics of each letter were somewhat specific to that particular church. However, the churches shared the letters with each other and collectively reaped the benefits of Paul's instruction and encouragement.

In Paul's first letter to the Church of Corinth, he asked the new Christians to serve each other in love and to be united in their faith. In chapter 2:16 of this first letter, Paul selected the Greek word *noun*[8] (a form of *nous*) to describe or define the good mind of Christ:

> "For who has known the mind of the Lord; who has advised him?" But we have the mind of Christ (1 Corinthians 2:16 NIV).

Did you get the point of this verse? Paul says that *we* (Christians) *have the mind of Christ*. Okay, now hold that thought ...

Paul wrote a second letter to the Church of Corinth about six months later. However, in this letter, he gets personal. Paul asked the church leadership to re-instate a penitent, Christian brother. To make his point on forgiveness, in chapter 2:11, Paul selects the Greek word *nohmata*[9] (a form of noema) commonly translated in this verse as "schemes."

Here is nohmata in context:

> [I]n order that Satan might not outwit us. For we are not unaware of his schemes (2 Cor. 2:11 NIV).

You are a Priest and a Warrior

Jeff, here is the interesting part. Like the carefully crafted word that Paul used in his letter to the Ephesians to describe Satan as The World-controller, this next Greek word also is not used very often in the Bible. In fact, it is only used five times by Paul in the New Testament (2 Cor. 2:11; 2 Cor. 3:14; 2 Cor. 4:4; 2 Cor. 11:3; and Php. 4:7). Now hang in there – we are almost to the "aha" moment.

This same Greek word *nohmata* is used by Paul in all five verses — to describe both man's natural or warrior mind AND to describe Satan's mind!

If you follow Paul's use and pattern of this word, then 2 Cor. 2:11 should read: *in order that Satan might not outwit us. For we are not unaware of his MIND.*

Void of Christ, our natural mind *is* the mind of Satan. These contrasting verses also explain why no one can be good or holy without the *good mind* of Jesus.

So take your time and choose your future wife and friends very carefully — choose those of "a like mind." When we surrender to Christ, we receive His mind and His Spirit. We become one of His children and the assurance that we will live with him in Heaven for all eternity. Only God's children enter heaven. Only God's Kingdom of priests are saved.

The Battle For Your Identity

The World-controller is a crafty and convincing liar. Did you know that *salvation by association* is not actually biblical? In the passage below from the Gospel of John, Jesus makes this point crystal clear as He spars with the Jewish Pharisees and their *salvation by association* thinking. As you will see, Christ's conclusion regarding their *real identity* is quite chilling.

> "I speak of what I have seen with my Father, and you do what you have heard from your father." They answered him, "Abraham is our father."
>
> Jesus said to them, "If you were Abraham's children, you would be doing the works Abraham did, but now you seek to kill me, a man who has told you the truth that I heard from God. This is not what Abraham did. You are doing the works YOUR father did."
>
> They said to him, "We were not born of sexual immorality. We have one Father even God."
>
> Jesus said to them, "If God were your Father, you would love me, for I came from God and I am here. I came not of my own accord, but he sent me. Why do you not understand what I say? It is because you cannot BEAR to hear my word.
>
> You are of YOUR father the devil, and your will is to do your father's desires. He was a murderer from the

> beginning, and does not stand in the truth, because there is no truth in him. When he lies, he speaks out of his own character, for he is a liar and the father of lies. But because I tell the truth, you do not believe me. Which one of you convicts me of sin? If I tell the truth, why do you not believe me?
>
> Whoever is of God hears the words of God. The reason why you do not hear them is that you are not of God" (John 8:38-47 ESV, emphasis added).

Jeff, in case you are wondering, you belong to God because you listen to Him. You belong to Him because you have His mind — his Holy Spirit is inside of you. This is the evidence of God's love and your adoption into His family:

> Whoever is of God, hears the words of God (John 8:47 ESV).

The Battle For Your Protection

The Apostle John records Jesus' detailed prayer on the night before His crucifixion. Filled with love and compassion, Jesus prays for his disciples and *all* who come after them — that they will know and listen to the Father through His Holy Spirit. Beginning with chapter 17:15 below, read how Jesus prays to Father God:

> "I don't ask you to take them out of the world, but to protect them from the Evil One. They do not belong to

the world, just as I do not belong to the world. Set them apart for holiness by means of the truth — your word is truth. Just as you sent me into the world, I have sent them into the world. On their behalf I am setting myself apart for holiness, so that they too may be set apart for holiness by means of the truth.

"I pray not only for these, but also for those who will trust in me because of their word, that they may all be one. Just as you, Father, are united with me and I with you,

"I pray that they may be united with us, so that the world may believe that you sent me.

"The glory which you have given to me, I have given to them; so that they may be one, just as we are one — I united with them and you with me, so that they may be completely one, and the world thus realize that you sent me, and that you have loved them just as you have loved me.

"Father, I want those you have given me to be with me where I am; so that they may see my glory, which you have given me because you loved me before the creation of the world. Righteous Father, the world has not known you, but I have known you, and these people have known that you sent me. I made your name known to them, and I will continue to make it known; so that the love with which you have loved me may be in them, and I myself may be united with them" (John 17:15-26 (ESV).

Win The Battle With The Good Mind Of Christ

Use your "Good Mind of Christ" to talk to God — then to do the will of God. I call this peculiar form of reasoning, "*prayer.*" If you are a Christian, then you believe in both a physical *and* a spiritual world — both with structure, rules and laws. Practically speaking, you work for real money, that buys real food, that is eaten by your hungry physical body. Likewise, you experience real "mental" pain and anguish from a hurtful remark spoken by a dear, old friend. When you make amends and forgive your friend then God restores real love, joy and peace in you. Both food and forgiveness are real. One nourishes your body and the other heals your Spirit. And both must be considered as you continually submit to God's will and purpose for your life.

After Christ's baptism, the Father publicly praised Him:

> "This is my Son, whom I love; with him I am well pleased" (Matt 3:17 NIV).

Then the Holy Spirit led Jesus into the desert to be tempted by Satan. He fasted for 40 days, and when He was at his weakest physical point, Satan unloaded his best tricks on him.

Warriors Know Their Enemy

He used his best temptations — the good ones — his tried and true arsenal that had tricked mankind for thousands of years. But they did not work on Jesus. He chose NOT to use his supernatural power to prove anything. His "mind of Christ" was able to clearly see the tricks and lies of the enemy. And now it is your turn.

Use your "mind of Christ" to see the tricks and lies of the enemy. Based on scriptures in the Bible, here is an abbreviated description of "what you are fighting."

What You Are Fighting[10]	
The Enemy, the World-controller, is also known as:	Satan
	The Serpent
	The Accuser
	The Adversary
	A murderer/father of lies
	Angel of the abyss
	Prince of demons
	The ruler of the powers of the air
	The prince of this world
	The god of this world
	The Wicked One
The Enemy manipulates our minds to:	Instigate evil
	Tempt man to sin
	Undo God's work
	Secure men's worship
	Make men turn away from God

What You Are Fighting	
The Enemy is an evil father to *his* children:	They do his will
	He blinds them
	He deceives them
	He troubles them
	They will all perish with him
Although we are God's children, Satan has the power to:	Tempt us
	Attack our health
	Accuse us
	Sift us
	Lead us astray
	Seize our property
	Believe his lying teachers
	To devour us
But as Christians we are to:	Beware of his schemes so that he does not trick us
	Fight against him
	Resist him
	Overcome him

Can you see how the true battle is in your mind, with your mind and for your mind? Although tired and hungry from fasting, Jesus remained a rock without sin. Jesus knew His enemy and ultimately won this battle of the minds and finished the job with his death and resurrection. Yes, indeed, he passed the test!

Pass Your Test With The Good Mind Of Christ

The *World-controller* uses the wedge of self-righteousness and the hammer of unforgiveness on Christians all the time. If that does not work, he will use jealousy, greed, power AND the hammer of judgment. But most of the enemy's flaming arrows are hidden in the quiver of PRIDE. Pride says, "No, that's not fair — I want it; give it to me."

Pride is a secretive sin. It hides behind holiness in most religions. I have seen Christians "take pride" in ridding themselves of sin. Although it sounds inconceivable that getting rid of sin can be sinful, it is actually a major strategy of the enemy. Again, Satan uses *pride* to cause us to believe in a different gospel — the "Gospel of Works" — which replaces God's grace with self-righteous legalism.

Therefore, self-righteous teaching should be *Number One* on your red flag list. Do not let any pastor, evangelist, religious teacher, friend or relative beat the self-righteous wedge into your right mind with their judgment hammer. Recognize this tactic of the enemy. It can crush your testimony and destroy your hope.

Jesus rebuked the self-righteous behavior of the Pharisees and Sadducees. He threatened their jobs, their societal position and their man-made ticket to heaven. So they turned on him. As we read in the Gospel of Mark:

> The Pharisees came and began to question Jesus. To test him, they asked him for a sign from heaven. He sighed deeply and said, "Why does this generation ask for a miraculous sign? I tell you the truth, no sign will be given to it." Then he left them, got back into the boat and crossed to the other side. The disciples had forgotten to bring bread, except for one loaf they had with them in the boat. "Be careful," Jesus warned them. "Watch out for the yeast of the Pharisees and that of Herod" (Mark 8:11-15 NIV).

Paul picked up where Jesus left off with this warning:

> You were running a good race. Who cut in on you and kept you from obeying the truth? That kind of persuasion does not come from the one who calls you. "A little yeast works through the whole batch of dough." I am confident in the Lord that you will take no other view. The one who is throwing you into confusion will pay the penalty, whoever he may be (Galatians 5:7-10 NIV).

Son, unfortunately "yeast teaching" is alive and well in the church today. From my perspective, there are three false teachings that are leading believers astray and trashing the Good News of the Gospel of Jesus Christ:

Warriors Know Their Enemy

1. "The politically correct Jesus" — The Gospel *like* me.

2. "Jesus is my genie" — The Gospel *for* me.

3. "No thanks, I'm good. I'll wash my own feet" — The Gospel *of* me.

A friend of mine once said that heresy is truth to an extreme. For some reason, when the solid foundations of your faith are broken, Satan accelerates his destruction with precision accuracy. That is why Chapter 10 is dedicated to the yeast teaching strategies of the enemy — specifically how he manipulates and destroys relationships.

His demons devour baby Christians like a pack of wolves hunting down a young calf. They quietly surround a young calf as it wanders off alone. Then at the right time they go for the kill. And after the feast, they hunt again. But this time they spot a proud old bull. A bull that still believes he can defeat any enemy alone and without the help of others.

Both the young and the old fall prey to Satan's schemes. Without Christ's protection, no one is completely safe. Even healthy adults can fall away if they get careless and ignore the sure signs of danger. So let the Holy Spirit clean you up *every day*, and allow a few, mature Christians into your life. Over time, they will tactfully point out "a blind spot" that needs to be addressed. Praise God when this happens and allow them to wash that dirty stain off your feet with a loving prayer.

Trust The Good News Of The Gospel

Redemption is the Good News of the Gospel – it is the hope of salvation and a pure definition of God's grace! You know the Good News. You have the mind of Christ. You have the power of the Holy Spirit to defend yourself against all the enemy's crafty schemes. Almighty God has given you his powerful armor to be a superconqueror who sheds His wonderful light in a world of darkness.

Lord Jesus, I pray that you hone my son's discernment — as sharp as a razor — to see the plans and evil schemes of the enemy. I also pray that he approaches life with the confidence of a warrior who is equipped with the armor of God to stand his ground with the power and courage of King David. Let him realize his identity in you, for you have overcome the world … and have already defeated the father of lies.

Chapter 5

The Power in Priests

Your Grandpa Norm invited me to a very special event fifteen years ago — his annual WWII Navy reunion.

When I arrived that evening, I noticed how the veterans interacted with each another. They talked about the good stuff and the funny stories, all the while it was obvious that no one was being politically correct. When your Grandpa Norm (or "Pop" as I called him) introduced me to a few of the guys, I glanced at their nametags and smiled. One said, "Red" and another "Dago." Pop's nametag said, "Shorty."

I asked Pop if he was upset about his nickname. He replied with a look of confusion, "Well no, son. Why should I? I'm short. That guy over there used to have bright, red hair, so he goes by 'Red.' And that guy's Italian, so we call him 'Dago.'" Then he laughed and continued telling stories until the formal program began. That is when the mood changed.

They stood at attention and saluted the American flag while saying the Pledge of Allegiance. Pop (and many others) cried

You are a Priest and a Warrior

when someone read the list of comrades from their battalion who had recently passed away.

They quickly perked up and continued their laughing and verbal abuse when they sat down for dinner. I sat next to Pop and witnessed it all. It was hilarious.

The joking slowed down after dinner when it was time to say goodbye. There were no words this time, only long hugs and short stares that seemed to whisper, "I'll see you next year or on the other side."

These former soldiers had a powerful union. Their bond was too strong to be easily offended — they understood the big picture and their role in it — and they did not sweat the small stuff. It was a bond that lasted a lifetime, and they proved it by proudly wearing their politically incorrect name badges all evening. I experienced a slice of history that night with humble, forgotten heroes.

After that, Norm finally opened up and talked about the war. Jeff, do you remember that day? Your mom sure does. She said that her dad never spoke about the war with anyone, but you were special and on *that* day he spoke about it to *you*!

Your Grandpa was in the Battle of Guadalcanal. He said it was terrible. He served our country as a Navy Corpsman — a Pharmacist First Mate (the Navy's version of a medic) — but on the front lines, everyone called him "Doc." He patched up a lot

The Power in Priests

of soldiers during that first year after Pearl Harbor, but nothing compared to the battle for Henderson Airfield in the Solomon Islands in October, 1942.

Many did not make it. His last act of kindness to them was to place their remains inside body bags and send these fallen heroes back home. No wonder he never talked about it.

But your grandpa had a very special relationship with you — so he opened up and talked away. As he used to say, "Jeff, I've got nine granddaughters and one grandson!"

Son, you and I also have a special relationship and a strong union. These types of father/son bonds do not happen overnight. In fact, they can take a lifetime to develop. For many years, I have enjoyed our discussions and activities together. First, I was your dad AND your personal coach. I recall that you did not like some of my coaching. Somehow, a few years later, my role changed from dad-and-coach to dad-and-friend.

I think you moved me into your "friend circle" when you asked me to go lift weights with you at the gym. As you pushed me hard on the weights, my mind drifted back a few years. I remembered the day you were born. Back then I imagined us lifting weights side-by-side and spotting each other on the bench press. I remembered looking at your tiny little body while sporting a huge smile. I knew I would have to wait a very long time, until a special day in the future, for this dream to be realized.

Thanks son, for asking me to "go lift" with you a few years ago. It was a very big deal to me and an almost forgotten dream come true.

I continue to marvel at your spiritual wisdom and your living testimony to the Lord. That is the evidence of your powerful union with God. So please read this chapter only as a reminder — a reminder to keep your union with God strong — to draw on His mighty strength as you fight with His power and armor.

Grow Powerful In Union With The Lord

> Finally, grow powerful in union with the Lord, in union with his mighty strength! Use all the armor and weaponry that God provides, so that you will be able to stand against the deceptive tactics of the Adversary (Ephesians 6:10, 11 CJB).

Paul ends his letter to the Ephesian church with a specific plan to fight and defeat the enemy. He encourages the church to *grow powerful with the Lord and to use all of His armor to fight the enemy.*

Son, you cannot fight Satan on your own. Therefore, you must be very intentional about strengthening your relationship with the Lord. You have to spend time with Him — in prayer and in Bible study. Like Pop and his war buddies, you have to go through a few battles with God to understand how He operates *with you* in a variety of situations.

The Power in Priests

As I stated in Chapter 1, you became a priest on the day you accepted Jesus Christ as your Lord and Savior. *The fact that you are a priest and a warrior is the most important aspect of this book.* It is the reason Jesus died on the cross — to redeem you and set you apart for HIS special purpose.

In Chapter 2, you learned that all men are born as warriors with an instinct to fight. But without the Holy Spirit, warriors fight for the wrong things. The priestly spirit directs the warrior to fight a new fight — a spiritual fight to advance the Kingdom of God. Together, the first two chapters answer the question, "Who am I?"

In Chapter 3, you learned *why* you are a priest and a warrior. Specifically, that you are part of a holy nation to serve God and His people. You have been set apart to serve and behave differently from the rest of the world as you allow the Holy Spirit to wash your feet and keep you clean. Jesus told Peter that he must allow Him to wash his feet — and then follow His example in sharing His love by doing the same.

Like Opa studied HIS enemy, in Chapter 4, I encouraged you to study YOUR enemy the *World-controller*, to discover who YOU are fighting:

> For we are not struggling against human beings, but against the rulers, authorities and cosmic powers governing this darkness, against the spiritual forces of evil in the heavenly realm (Ephesians 6:12 CJB).

You are a Priest and a Warrior

Son, you are a superconqueror — strong in the Lord and equipped with His Holy Spirit, His armor, and His weaponry.

> So take up every piece of war equipment God provides; so that when the evil day comes, you will be able to resist; and when the battle *is won*, you will still be standing (Ephesians 6:13 CJB, emphasis added).

Now that you know *who* and *what* you are fighting, put on the armor of God and WIN — As described below in Ephesians 6:14-18 (CJB).

Tell The Truth

> Therefore, stand! Have the belt of truth buckled around your waist (Ephesians 6:14a CJB).

Before you start swinging away, stop and pray about your approach. Think about your situation and be honest with yourself — what is the truth? Then begin your "fight" with truth buckled around your waist — to hold up your pants.

If you fight without the belt of truth — your pants will drop to your feet. You will end up exposed and humiliated like some of today's politicians, athletes and corporate executives.

Knowing the truth about who you are and what you believe is the anchor of your soul. This strong conviction prepares you for, and protects you from, risky situations that spring up in front of you.

Thankfully, you already know this fundamental principle of the Gospel – that *truth* is always tested with a True or False test — it is always just one or the other — and that is the truth about truth!

Be Righteous

> [P]ut on righteousness for a breastplate (Ephesians 6:14b CJB).

Righteousness is right behavior. Think of your new name as "Jeff Jesus," and then behave and act like a priest. I cannot stress this enough, without *truth* and *righteousness*, you do not have a chance of winning God's way.

Tell Your Story

> [A]nd wear on your feet the readiness that comes from the Good News of shalom (Ephesians 6:15 CJB).

The enemy will manipulate friends, family and acquaintances to test your testimony. Inevitably, a circumstance will develop where you must convey your version of "truth" — to explain the Gospel according to Jeff, so to speak.

You will be forced to pass this test in front of witnesses on Earth and in Heaven. When this happens, you must trust God and rely on the Holy Spirit to speak "truth" on your behalf.

In high school, you listened to the Holy Spirit and reached out to a few, lonely classmates and neighborhood boys that needed a friend. You picked them up in our suburban and took them to the church youth group every Sunday night. Your mom and I watched you invest in these young men. *You passed the test.*

When you were a freshman in college, you asked me to lead a cigar-smoking Bible study on the back patio — you called it, "Holy Smokes." I remember thinking to myself, "What a great idea!" Your unconventional Bible study did the trick. We had fun smoking cigars *and* learning about the Good News of the Gospel. *You passed the test.*

Then, you stood your ground that first year in Boston when your fellow salesmen challenged your faith and your Christian testimony. You told the truth about the Gospel of Jesus Christ. Even though the stakes were high, God was faithful and He honored your testimony. Again, *you passed the test.*

Son, you will have many tests like these in your life. Always remember that Jesus *is* the Good News that brings all aspects of shalom to EVERYONE! There is nothing to fear. Stand confidently and share *your personal testimony* — your personal story of your peace and heavenly assurance.

Trust God

> Always carry the shield of trust — with which you will be able to extinguish all the flaming arrows of the Evil One (Ephesians 6:16 CJB).

Most Bible translations say, "The shield of faith." But I like the CJB translation a little better as it seems more personal to me. I have faith in a lot of things, but in battle, I need to *trust God* — that HE has my back. I need to count on HIS many promises from the Bible — to trust that He will never leave me.

Protect Your Head

> And take the helmet of deliverance (Ephesians 6:17a CJB).

Do not let anything or anyone mess with your head. Protect it! Protect the hope and security of your salvation. In Chapter 10, you will see how the enemy works on your mind to steal your hope and destroy your relationships — especially your bond with Jesus.

Use Your Sword

> [A]long with the sword given by the Spirit, that is, the Word of God (Ephesians 6:17b CJB).

You will also take action with the sword of the Spirit in the next chapter: *Warriors Take Action*. The sword of the Spirit is your *best* offensive weapon. It is the Word of God spoken through you. It is *effective* and *powerful*. So use it to move forward, on the right path, in the Kingdom of God.

The Power Of Prayer

> [A]s you pray at all times, with all kinds of prayers and requests, in the Spirit, vigilantly and persistently, for all God's people (Ephesians 6:18 CJB).

John Owen, the British theologian that I mentioned in Chapter 1, lived during the age of Milton, Rembrandt and Sir Isaac Newton. He was the Vice Chancellor of Oxford and a close advisor to King Charles I, King Charles II and Richard Cromwell during a turbulent time in history. While England was at war with Scotland, France and Holland in 1662, the church leaders seized religious power and expelled more than 2,000 puritan clergy from their churches. Then the "great plague" killed 20 percent of London's population in 1665. In 1666, the entire city burned to the ground. Over a 30-year period (from 1645-75), Owen buried his wife and ten children! Only one of his daughters survived[11]. In 1673, he published a book, *A Discourse on The Holy Spirit* — an inspired manuscript on the workings and nature of the Holy Spirit. Think about the pain and suffering he experienced while you read this section (on prayer) from his book:

The whole work of faith is denominated from the duty of prayer, for it is said, *"whoever shall call on the name of the Lord, shall be saved," Rom. 10:13*. No heart can conceive what treasures of mercy are contained in this great privilege, of having liberty and ability to approach God at all times. This is the relief, the weapons, and the refuge of the Church, in all conditions.

It is our duty to make use of this gift of the Spirit. Have you an ability to pray always freely given you by the Holy Ghost, why do you not pray always, in private, in families, as occasions offer? Prayer is that singular duty, in which every grace is acted, every sin opposed, every blessing obtained; the whole of our obedience is concerned in it, and much of our present and future blessedness depends upon it.

What difficulties and discouragements rise up against it, what aversion there is in corrupted nature to it, what distractions often attend it is well known to the people of God, but to help us under our various infirmities; to give us freedom and confidence in coming to the throne; to enable us as children to cry, Abba Father, the Holy Spirit is given to us.

Who then can express the sin and folly of neglecting prayer? How does it grieve the Spirit, and injure our own souls! Can we go from day to day in the neglect of opportunities and occasions of prayer? How shall we answer this contempt of the Spirit's gracious aid? Do carnal persons habitually live without prayer? Alas! They know not how to pray; but for those who have received this gift of the Spirit, enabling them to pray, and making it pleasant to the inner man — how great an aggravation is it to their sin! I press this duty of prayer the more, because the temptations and dangers of the present day particularly call for it.

You are a Priest and a Warrior

If we were to talk less and pray more, things would be better than they are in the world.

It is the duty of those who have received this gift — to cherish it — to stir it up and improve it; it is freely bestowed, but it is carefully to be preserved. It is a gospel-talent given to be traded with and thereby increased. And this is to be done.[12]

Son, although my faith has been tested many times, I have never faced real adversity like that of John Owen — or like that of my parents and grandparents during the Great Depression and both world wars.

Owen urged all believers to pray often for each other and for everything. He said, "Prayer is the relief, the weapons, and the refuge of the Church, in all conditions."

Then he ended with, "And this is to be done!"

Chapter 6

Warriors Take Action

Okay, it is time to finish Opa's story. After a decade of studying Hitler he finally made up his mind, it was time to go. Opa *took action* and moved Oma, my mom and my aunt to New York in April, 1939. Because of his timing and preparation, he was able to move all of his household goods to America — just before all hell broke loose.

Somewhere along the line, my Jewish forefathers in Holland heard the Good News of the Gospel and converted to Christianity. Why else would Opa have a 1901 American Standard Bible? Also, when I was a kid, my mom use to say that they attended a Presbyterian church in Holland and again in New York. Although Opa and Oma were Protestant Dutch citizens, they had Jewish blood in their veins — and Hitler wanted blood!

Jeff, *one* month after they arrived in America, the German ocean liner *SS St. Louis*[13] with about 1000 Jewish passengers, was blocked from entering Cuba or any other country.

This tragic event was broadcast around the world. From that point on, it was nearly impossible for Jews to flee Europe. The *St. Louis* was stranded at sea for a month — even the United States turned them away. When all hope was lost, the ship returned to Germany. Upon its arrival, the Jewish passengers were shuffled away and subsequently sent to concentration camps.

On September 1, 1939, Germany invaded Poland. Two days later, Great Britain declared war on Germany. On November 30, 1939, Finland fell. Four months later, both Denmark and Norway were conquered. Ignoring their standing position of neutrality, on May 10, 1940, just 13 months after Opa's departure, the Germans marched right into Holland.

Although the Dutch fought bravely, they were no match for the Nazi army and surrendered just five days later. Shortly thereafter, Jewish assets were seized and the Jews began to be transported to concentration camps.

Just *one day* before the Dutch surrendered, on May 14, 1940, my Great Uncle Theo (Oma's brother) escaped from Holland on a small, Dutch fishing boat with his wife and two sons. Unlike Opa, they left everything behind, including three of my great grandparents who died in Auschwitz in 1942. It is hard to think about this, let alone write about it.

But Uncle Theo's family escaped — that is the good news! They landed in England and worked their way to America via Canada.

It is unbelievable that they survived and had been living in New York since the war.

I met Uncle Theo's grandson, Maury, for the first time in November, 2011, just two months after I received cousin Joey's "We are Jewish" phone call (the call that I mentioned back in Chapter 1). On that November day, Maury, Joey and I exchanged stories and pictures as we assembled the puzzle of our family's lives into one, amazing story.

Son, Opa studied his enemy *and* took action. He made the bold and courageous decision to move across the U-boat infested Atlantic and into America — a sanctuary for the persecuted; a country without a king or a dictator; a country founded on Mosaic Law; one nation under God that *was* and *is* doing God's work throughout the world.

Get Your Mind Ready For Work

> Therefore, get your minds ready for work, keep yourselves under control, and fix your hopes fully on the gift you will receive when Yeshua the Messiah is revealed (1 Peter 1:13 CJB).

I chose the Complete Jewish Bible (CJB) translation because it seems to convey Peter's thinking a little better. Peter gets right to the point as he introduces *action* and a sense of urgency into this letter. In one powerful verse, he gives us three commands that summarize the work of a superconqueror:

- Get your minds ready for work.
- Keep yourselves under control.
- Fix your hopes fully on the gift you will receive when Yeshua the Messiah is revealed.

Did you notice the preparation theme in this verse? It sounds like the mental preparation that you do before a football game, a boxing match or a military battle. Peter encourages you to thoroughly prepare your mind for *action* — to do the work of the Lord. Prepare to live God's way as a priest and a warrior. Keep yourself under control, alert and ready to answer God's call with, "I'm all in."

Keep Yourselves Under Control

Exactly what does this mean? Rather than speculating, in the next few verses Peter explains *how* we are to keep ourselves under control. But prepare yourself, it may not be what you think.

> As people who obey God, do not let yourselves be shaped by the evil desires you used to have when you were still ignorant. On the contrary, following the Holy One who called you, become holy yourselves in your entire way of life; since the Tanakh says, "You are to be holy because I am holy" (1 Peter 1:14-16 CJB).

Son, it is important to remember that Peter is writing to *all* Christians. With that said, he begins verse 14 with a subtle reminder of who *we* are — "people who obey God." Then he continues in verses 14-16 with a command for holy living.

This is the point I have been making — that if you call yourself a Christian, then the topic of holiness cannot be ignored. Since you are not immature any longer, be alert and do not let your old mind of Satan influence your behavior. Follow your High Priest, Yeshua the Messiah, and become holy in your entire way of life. If you need to change your lifestyle, then do it! And do it because God the Father said, *"You are to be holy because I am holy."*

Peter is not pushing a "try harder" message. It is actually the opposite. It is a decision to *let go*, and allow the Holy Spirit to take over. Son you already know this — you know that the Holy Spirit is the guide and the author of all of your plans.

As I mentioned in the last chapter, God does not send you out into the world without spiritual weapons or training. First, He trains you by watching you in difficult situations. Then, after you have passed a few tests, He moves you on to maturity with more spiritual responsibility, power and authority in Christ.

This is exactly what Peter is trying to convey. All of this is called "self-control" — the discipline of leaving your old way of life behind and allowing the Holy Spirit to change you — to make you holy for God's Kingdom work.

"Being holy" allows you to hear from God. If you hear from God, then you will know what to do and when to do it. When you say, "I just don't know what to do," stop and pray. Ask God to tell you what is wrong. If you sinned, then repent (with all your heart), and quickly get back on track. If it is a test, then pray and wait for God's answer. *In all cases*, pray every day and fine-tune your spiritual hearing, then you will hear clearly from God.

Jesus defined *being holy* for all mankind by His willful and obedient action on the cross. It was not His title, "Lord" that saved you from death and separation from God, it was his obedient action on the cross that saved you. Jesus is your example. You must be holy in your mind and in your actions — in your thoughts and in your deeds.

As I mentioned in Chapter 3, this can only be accomplished through the sanctifying work of the Holy Spirit. God will never force you to do anything. He will only ask you to obey. As it is written, "*Be holy, because I am Holy.*" No wiggle room.

Fix Your Hopes Fully On The Gift

What are you hoping for? Sometimes the obvious questions are the hardest to answer. When I was around your age, I am not sure that I thought much about Heaven. It seemed far away. Instead, I hoped for short-term things that would provide a better quality of life now. That does not sound very spiritual, but it is probably the truth. I suppose there is a balance here. It is good to pray for simple things — that God will bless you and your family, protect you from evil, and so forth. Otherwise, you might become too heavenly-minded to be of any earthly good to God or anyone else — I think that is how the saying goes.

However, it is important to keep your eyes focused on the prize as you go about your Kingdom work — because the work of a superconqueror is hard. Peter and Paul compare it to being an alien in this world. Perhaps they really meant an alien from another planet. (Maybe that is not too far-fetched!)

Once again, the lifestyle of a Christian is not popular in the world around us. I often feel like I do not belong anywhere. But I know who I am (in Christ), and best of all, where I am going!

But our country is changing. We may encounter real persecution in the very near future. I will not speculate on its form, but it is possible that we might lose the original alignment of God's laws with our nation's constitutional laws. If that were to happen, would America still be the land of the free and the home of the brave? I am not so sure. So fix your hopes on the gift now, and paint an indelible picture of Heaven in your right mind of Christ. That was Jesus' suggestion to Peter and the disciples on the night before His crucifixion.

> Let not your hearts be troubled. Believe in God; believe also in me. In my Father's house are many rooms. If it were not so, would I have told you that I go to prepare a place for you? And if I go and prepare a place for you, I will come again and will take you to myself, that where I am you may be also (John 14:1-3 ESV).

Son, believe Jesus. Hold on to His promise. Put your trust in God the Father, God the Son, and God the Holy Spirit. And fix your eyes on the prize, which comes with your very own room in Heaven!

Chapter 7

Priests Praise God

> Through Jesus, therefore, let us continually offer to God a sacrifice of praise - the fruit of lips that confess his name (Hebrews 13:15 NIV).

Son, I am not proud to admit it but this verse does not actually describe me. Truthfully, when things do not go well, I do not offer praise to God. Perhaps there are a lot of Christians out there like me.

With this confession, I would like to tell you a story about someone else — a story of sacrifice and love from a person that has praised God through thick and thin. Jeff, this person is your mom, Cindi. The story is about how she witnessed the fruit from a lifelong prayer to see both of her parents receive the gift of salvation in the final seasons of their lives.

For many years your mom watered the "seed of life" inside of you with Christ's love and encouragement. That was her life's work as a stay-at-home mom. As it was then and is still today, she walks the talk. She lives outside of her comfort zone. She lives a sacrificial life that is full of interruptions and inconveniences, and you and your sisters are living proof of it. You are *the fruit* — the fruit of lips that confess the name of Jesus.

Cindi also watered the dormant seeds in her parents' shallow soil with the same living water of Jesus Christ. Isn't that our job? — first sharing the Gospel with our immediate family and then with everyone else?

If you recall in Chapter 5, I mentioned that the *Power in Priests* comes from the Holy Spirit and from putting on the armor of God. Here are a couple of those verses:

> [A]nd wear on your feet the readiness that comes from the Good News of shalom. And always carry the shield of trust (Ephesians 6:15-16 CJB).

That is what we are supposed to do — listen to the Holy Spirit's direction, always be ready with the Good News of Shalom, and then trust God with the outcome! It is not up to you or anyone else whether or not a person decides to follow Jesus. Son, you cannot save anyone — that is up to God. Your job is to pray, hope and testify!

That is why I am documenting *this story* — a story that you already know. However, I am not telling this story to brag about anyone. This story is a *real* example of faith and hope in action, or as Hebrews 13:15 says, "The fruit of lips that confessed His name." As you know, your mom prayed and shared the Good News about Jesus with your grandparents for over three, long decades.

But you should also know that many others were also praying for your grandparents. This is important so that no one can boast or take credit for their salvation. Again, that is up to God.

Jeff, as you remember, your Grandma and Grandpa loved you and all of their grandkids. Whenever possible they made an effort to spend time with their family. When they were not with us, they were with their neighbors or playing cards with friends. They were open-minded about many things, except one — Jesus Christ.

During their visits to see us in Seattle and Dallas, they often accepted our invitation to join us at church. It was uncomfortable at times, especially when they heard a challenging message from the pulpit.

Year after year we prayed, but sadly, they always left without making a decision for Christ. I began to lose faith. I thought, "It's never gonna happen."

But your mom never lost hope. Whether in person or on the phone with them, Cindi was always kind, always patient, and always gracious and loving. And she prayed that God would keep them alive long enough to hear and receive the Good News of the Gospel so they could be with us in Heaven for all eternity.

She prayed that God would bring someone at the right moment when they would be open to hear some Good News about God.

In 2006, 33 years after your mom accepted the Lord, your 83-year-old grandma called with bad news. The doctor said that her emphysema was rapidly advancing. So we prayed and then moved to Boise to help your Aunt Sue take care of your grandparents.

A few months after we arrived, your mom began to gently discuss God and Heaven with your grandma. Then one day, God spoke to your mom with a sense of urgency — it was time to get bold.

Once again she had a loving conversation with your grandma, but this time it was different; this time your grandma listened carefully.

They joined us at church a few weeks later to hear our minister explain the Gospel in a way that made sense to them. The next day, your grandma called your mom to tell her that she had made a decision to follow Jesus. She said, "Honey, better late than never."

And Jeff, your Grandpa Norm also made a decision for Christ. For him it was a decision to come back to God, having left the faith due to the evil he experienced in WWII. What an amazing answer to decades of prayer!

Priests Praise God

At 85 and 86 years old, they signed up and attended the new believers' class at our church. Every week they would slowly walk into the classroom with their Bibles in one hand while pulling their oxygen tanks with the other.

Their health was failing fast so we treasured every moment with them over the next two years. And when it was time they peacefully passed away to be with the Lord — first your grandpa and then your grandma, eight months later.

Son, as I look back, your mom praised God in the good years and in the challenging ones. She showed us how to win God's way — with faith, hope and by sharing the love of Jesus with her parents, over a period of decades and right up to the very end.

Priests Praise God In All Situations

> Through Jesus, therefore, let us continually offer to God a sacrifice of praise -- the fruit of lips that confess his name (Hebrews 13:15 CJB).

When I read this verse I think of our duty to pray and praise God in all circumstances, but it is hard to actually do it. So, among other things, when I am down-and-out, I read the Psalms. It helps — or better said, they help to get me back on track.

The Book of Psalms contains 150 separate songs, poems, prayers and praises from every victorious and defeated season of David's life. Take a moment to read one of my favorites —

You are a Priest and a Warrior

Psalm 145, as David illustrates how to praise God in all situations.

> I will exalt you, my God the King; I will praise your name forever and ever. Every day I will praise you and extol your name forever and ever. Great is the LORD and most worthy of praise; his greatness no one can fathom.
>
> One generation will commend your works to another; they will tell of your mighty acts. They will speak of the glorious splendor of your majesty, and I will meditate on your wonderful works.
>
> They will tell of the power of your awesome works, and I will proclaim your great deeds. They will celebrate your abundant goodness and joyfully sing of your righteousness. The LORD is gracious and compassionate, slow to anger and rich in love.
>
> The LORD is good to all; he has compassion on all he has made. All you have made will praise you, O LORD; your saints will extol you.
>
> They will tell of the glory of your kingdom and speak of your might, so that all men may know of your mighty acts and the glorious splendor of your kingdom. Your kingdom is an everlasting kingdom, and your dominion endures through all generations.

Priests Praise God

The LORD is faithful to all his promises and loving toward all he has made. The LORD upholds all those who fall and lifts up all who are bowed down. The eyes of all look to you, and you give them their food at the proper time. You open your hand and satisfy the desires of every living thing.

The LORD is righteous in all his ways and loving toward all he has made. The LORD is near to all who call on him, to all who call on him in truth. He fulfills the desires of those who fear him; he hears their cry and saves them.

The LORD watches over all who love him, but all the wicked he will destroy. My mouth will speak in praise of the LORD. Let every creature praise his holy name forever and ever (Psalm 145 NIV).

PRAISE THE NAME OF THE LORD

Isn't this an awesome proclamation? This particular psalm was written as an acrostic[14]. David used each letter of the Hebrew alphabet in succession, to start every phrase — as he praised and worshipped God with all of his heart, soul and mind.

Tough times require the unnatural discipline to worship and praise our Lord and Savior everyday for who He is, what He has done, and how He cares for us. It also takes courage. As you will read in the next chapter, you will use the courage from God and

You are a Priest and a Warrior

His Spirit of power, love and self-discipline to overcome all of life's discouragements.

We know from the Bible that David finished well. With that in mind, let us take a look at his last Psalm in the Bible — one last truth — one short sentence:

> Let everything that has breath praise the Lord. Praise the Lord! (Psalm 150:6 NIV, emphasis added).

Think of everything in Creation — every breathing miracle praising the Lord — as you read this list of names taken from the Bible, each one describing *the amazing Lord we praise.*

Names of God taken from the Bible[15].	
The Lord Who Provides	Judge
The Lord Who Heals	LORD
The Lord Our Banner	King
The Lord Who Sanctifies	Lawgiver
The Lord Our Peace	Light
he LORD Our God	Most High
The Lord Our Righteousness	Rock
The Great I AM	Rock of Israel
Everlasting God	Rock of My Refuge
The Mighty One of Jacob	Rock of My Salvation
Shepherd of Israel	Redeemer
Ancient of Days	The First and The Last
Our Creator	The Alpha and THE Omega
Our Deliverer	Our Father

Priests Praise God

Names of God taken from the Bible[15].	
Our Advocate	Our Papa
Holy One	Our Dad

You Are A Sacrifice Of Praise

David praised God when he was young and when he was old. He praised God when he was living in a cave and when he lived in a palace. He praised God before, during and after a battle. He relied on God continually. He praised God with his harp, his voice, his poems, his songs and his life. David is an excellent example of someone who praised God in many situations. His life was a kind of "first fruits" — a temporal, living "sacrifice of praise," announcing the One to come.

The Old Testament priests burned the first fruits of their crops as *thank offerings* to God. Then the high priests took the blood of sacrificed animals into the Holy of Holies and poured it out before the Lord. This sacrifice of praise temporarily washed away their sins. Then they took the dead and empty carcass *outside* the temple community and *outside the gates* and burned it before the Lord.

Jesus died outside the city of Jerusalem. It was His final sacrifice of praise. He was our example of how to live outside of our comfort zone — outside of our boundaries and predictable existence as a sacrifice of praise to the Father. But remember that Jesus died in our place so that we could live as superconquerors, now and for all eternity.

Son, I began this chapter with a wonderful story about your mother and how she never gave up hope and faithfully prayed for her parent's salvation. Then I added that your mom was a great example of what it means to BE a living sacrifice of praise — and that her parents were the *fruit of lips* that confessed the name of Jesus.

Well, there is more to the story.

Shortly after your Grandpa Norm passed away in December, 2009, your mother felt prompted by the Holy Spirit to write a short book and to teach a small group of women certain truths about Christianity. While still grieving the recent loss of her dad, and while helping your grieving grandma, she somehow finished her book in record time in February, 2010.

At the same time, two groups of women approached her asking if she would lead a study for them. Neither group had yet to decide on a book or topic. It became obvious to both group leaders that Cindi should teach the material from her new book. So she led *two*, seven-week studies in the dining room of our home.

Before it started, one of the women asked Cindi is she could bring a friend who had terminal cancer and who did not know Jesus. "Of course it's ok," replied your mom.

Priests Praise God

And through the Word of God, the study materials, and through the love of the other Christian women (and of course the promptings of the Holy Spirit), that woman accepted the Lord and was finally filled with God's peace.

Later, she mentioned to Cindi that she was no longer afraid to die; she was ready to meet Jesus in Heaven.

In those two studies, your mom taught with all of her heart. She loved all of the women as Christ did. And she wrote a great, unpublished book. Here are a few paragraphs from the chapter on *hope*:

I believe at the heart of every Christian woman (men too) is the hope that we are making a difference — for the better in our marriages, in our homes, as mothers, and in all of our relationships.

We've heard the expression, "We hope they're better off for having known us." But how does that apply to us as believers?

It's so much more than good friendships, good fellowship, or good advice — all of which are valuable.

One of my favorite verses in the Book of Isaiah, reminds me of what it's like to be a woman who shares hope. Let's read Chapter 61:1-3 NIV together:

The Spirit of the Sovereign Lord is on me, because the Lord has anointed me to preach good news to the poor. He has sent me to bind up the brokenhearted to proclaim freedom to the captives and release from darkness for the prisoners, to proclaim the year of the LORD'S favor and the day of vengeance of our God.

The chapter goes on to describe *the exchanges* that are made by the Spirit of our Sovereign Lord:

- A crown of beauty instead of ashes;
- The oil of gladness instead of mourning;
- And a garment of praise instead of a spirit of despair.

Of course, these exchanges apply to all of us — but we must share them — we can and should be extending the message of beauty and gladness — to everyone around us — all the time.

There is nothing sadder than seeing a person filled with complete hopelessness or despair. Anyone around you need the Good News? How about the brokenhearted — know anyone like that? I know some that are captive — held tightly by the enemy. Do you? We must commit to pray often — to be those vessels that influence everyone around us — with Christ's message of hope.

Son, your mother's words are inspiring. Your mom spent a lot of time with those women over that three-month period. She also spent a lot of time with your grandma since her health was rapidly failing.

Your mother pressed on. Then in July, 2010, your grandma passed away — just eight months after her husband. A few months later, Cindi's new friend with cancer also slipped away to be with God.

It was a sad *and* joyful year. I think that is the best way to say it. Although we were sad, we praised God that all of them had God's peace until the end!

Son, your mom praised God with her sacrificial living and God accepted it. He accepted her living sacrifice of praise! And in His mercy and grace, she received what she was hoping for. Son, that is how the sacrifice of praise — in faith, with hope, and through Christ's love — produces *fruit* — everlasting fruit in Heaven.

As it is written:

> Through Jesus, therefore, let us continually offer to God a sacrifice of praise --the fruit of lips that confess his name (Hebrews 13:15 NIV).

Chapter 8

Warriors Have Courage

> For God has not given us a spirit of cowardice, but of power and love and self-discipline (2 Timothy 1:7 LEB).

The Apostle Paul asked young Timothy to perform many difficult tasks including teaching large groups, leading older men and recruiting elders. It must have been intimidating. Therefore, Paul encouraged him to rely on God's Spirit of power, love and self-discipline.

Son, you have courage! It took tremendous courage to leave Boise and sell security systems, door-to-door, in Boston and New York over those two college summers. You experienced rejection all day long and every day, but you persevered.

You also shared your faith with your colleagues and a few prospects who did not buy a security system. One was a lonely, old man. You called me the next day and told me all about him. You said right up front that you knew he was not going to buy anything, but you still stayed and talked to him. Jeff, when you told me what happened, I was so proud of you. You listened patiently to the stories of a man who longed for, maybe even prayed for a friend.

As you left his house, you probably took a deep breath — knowing you had to get back to the door-to-door sales, and back to rejection. Son, I do not think I could have done it. But God gave you His Spirit of courage to conquer a GIANT called "discouragement."

God Gives Us A Spirit Of Courage

Before he became king, David was a shepherd — chosen by God and filled with the Holy Spirit at a fairly young age. You can read all about his early life beginning in 1 Samuel 16.

God used David's natural ability, intellect and life experiences to win his first battle against Goliath. Amazingly, the Spirit of God gave him courage to shout and claim the victory — *before* it happened!

But did David really kill a giant, or is this story just a fairy tale?

While playing golf a few years ago, one of my close, Christian friends laughed at the Goliath story. I do not recall how the topic came up, but I was shocked when he said, "So you think a teenage shepherd sprinted past the King of Israel and his entire army, and with his little sling and a tiny rock took out a nine-foot giant — a complete bull's-eye right on the forehead? Seriously? You really believe that?"

You are a Priest and a Warrior

Son, when my friend said that, I was quiet. Although I personally believed the story, I was stunned by the mocking spirit behind his comment and did not even try to defend myself or my faith.

The David and Goliath story is in the Bible and it was written by the Prophet Samuel, not David. If you are a Christian then you should believe this story and *all* of the documented stories in the Bible. Otherwise you become a "pick and choose" Christian who does not need the power or the courage of God for anything.

However, after that day on the golf course and to better defend my faith to my "Christian" friends, I did my own additional research and subsequently concluded that *for David*, that bull's-eye was very possible. I will provide support for my statement, first with a story from my childhood, and then with some highly relevant research that will appeal to your cognitive reasoning. Okay, now for the story.

In some ways, growing up in Southern California in the sixties was like living in my very own theme park. In the summer, like all the other boys, I would leave my house early in the morning and *maybe* return in time for dinner. I can still hear my mom yelling, "Richieeeeee, dinnerrrrrrr!" — or hear the relays from the neighborhood moms that echoed her mighty-call down the street and around the block.

Back then there was always something to do — from making a fort in a vacant lot, to playing tag at a friend's house. But most of the time, you would find me in my *own* backyard playing "dirt clods" with my younger brother Timmy.

When I was little, the stream behind our house overflowed almost every year. So the county transformed the creek into a narrow, concrete water channel with smooth vertical walls. Everyone called it "the wash." The excavation process produced thousands of small dirt clods that remained in our backyard for years.

For fun, we threw dirt clods at targets on the other side of the wash (about 20 yards away). We made up games and competed for candy like Starbursts, a piece of Bazooka Bubble Gum, or the grand prize where the loser had to do the winner's chores for the day. Timmy was a good shot and our games were competitive, so we played "dirt clods" all the time.

When Little League Baseball came along one of our coaches asked, "Who wants to pitch?" We all just stared at him. Then, remembering that we were only eight years old, one of the dads took us to the pitcher's mound and asked if anyone could hit *that* target (the catcher's glove) with *this* baseball. "Hmmm, dirt clods," I thought. So I stepped up to the mound, grabbed the ball and fired it right at the glove. I pitched for the next seven years.

Now back to the David and Goliath story. Jeff, what do you think it was like to be David the shepherd boy back then? Let us think through this. According to 1 Samuel 16:10, David was the youngest of eight boys. Yes, you heard that correctly; the poor kid had seven older brothers!

Since I am also from a large family (3 brothers and 3 sisters), I would guess that David's brothers made him watch the sheep all the time. If he had any spare time, they probably made him do their chores — and slapped him around if he did them poorly. And naturally, they threatened him if he even thought of going over their heads and complaining to their dad.

So my guess is that David just sucked it up while sitting alone for years, watching the family's sheep. I have heard that tending sheep is actually pretty boring, except for an occasional wolf raid.

He must have passed the time by playing his harp, singing songs and hitting targets with his sling. He probably did this everyday for about seven or eight years. As he grew, I suppose he moved from hitting stationary targets to killing wild animals — big ones!

Wolves, lions and bears were plentiful in the land of Zion in those days. In fact, David mentioned to King Saul, "Your servant has killed both the lion and the bear."[16]

God used those early years to train David for something big. Facing Goliath would take supernatural courage — or be the death wish of a crazy fool. King Saul knew that any serious challenger to the Philistine giant must have size, strength and years of hand-to-hand combat experience to have even a remote chance of staying alive. But God knew David's heart — and his years of slinger experience killing moving targets that could *eat him* if he missed!

Okay, but what about that amazing shot with that little rock? To put this in context, I am going to compare David's shot to a baseball's velocity, so hang in there while I walk you through it.

Major League pitchers throw a five ounce baseball about 100 mph or 146 feet per second over a distance of 60 feet, 6 inches (about 20 yards). As all baseball players know, a catcher's throw from home plate to second base is twice that distance.

Hypothetically, if a catcher threw, instead of a baseball, a five-ounce rock *twice* as fast as a pitcher and accidentally hit a base runner on his unprotected head, wouldn't *that* rock at *that* speed *permanently* take out the runner?

In a research study called, *The Sling, Forgotten Firepower of Antiquity*, the author states:

> The sling is mankind's second oldest projectile weapon after the spear, and it is still in use today. Simple, cheap, easy to make and lethally effective at surprisingly long range, the sling is found almost everywhere in the world. As is the case with most simple weapons, its only drawback is the amount of time necessary to attain mastery of technique.

Jeff, the study goes on to describe the history of the sling and illustrates, with pictures and diagrams, its use as a long-range weapon in battle. In a section called, *Sling Ballistics*, they recorded the velocity-on-impact and stopping power of various sized stones hurled at different speeds at targets set from 40-200 yards away. Here is another quote:

> It takes an impact energy of about 70 foot-pounds to cause a fracture of most bones of the human body, but less than 2 foot-pounds to pierce the human body. A 2-ounce projectile traveling at 200 feet per second will have an impact energy of 82 foot-pounds. It is generally agreed that on impact, sling stones could easily penetrate the body of an unarmored man.

Son, after a page of formulas and number crunching, here is what they concluded (emphasis added):

> … which gives us an impact … which exceeds that of a .357 Magnum at the muzzle. No wonder the sling in skilled hands was such a fearsome weapon. <u>Goliath had just as much chance against David as any Bronze Age warrior with a sword would have had against an adolescent armed – with a .45 [caliber] automatic pistol.</u>[17]

What else can I say? Empowered by the Holy Spirit, God used young David — an ordinary kid with unique skills and experience to slay Goliath. And Jeff, God continues *today*, to use ordinary people with unusual skills to do extraordinary things.

God Gives Us A Spirit Of Power

Now, God is asking *you* to stand firm with courage and power to share the Good News of the Gospel. This is no small task. Unfortunately, it takes tremendous courage to live as a priest and a warrior in 21st century America.

Political correctness is America's new religion and it makes cowards of Christian men. Political correctness turns holy priests and confident warriors into hypocrites. It turns Christian businessmen into "Zen masters" who say "God" instead of "Jesus" or wish people "Happy Holidays" instead of "Merry Christmas."

Was David politically correct when he claimed the victory for his living God in front of Goliath, the Philistine army and all of Israel? Was Peter politically correct on the Day of Pentecost when he stood in front of the crowd and fearlessly testified that Jesus Christ, whom they had crucified, was actually the Messiah?

Political correctness is a cancer. It dulls the sword of the Spirit and unplugs the power of God!

Son, resist the temptation to be politically correct and doctrinally incorrect when Christian topics surface in any conversation. I am not saying that you should pick a fight, but it is your duty to speak up and take a side.

Think of it this way: if you are known as a Christian, again, *if* you are known as a Christian, *and* you agree to a politically correct statement that contradicts the Word of God, then aren't you, by inference, a false teacher?

I know what I am saying — it is risky — especially in a business setting (yep, I have done it). Nevertheless, have courage and listen to the Holy Spirit's gentle direction. Then, *in love*, offer a Spirit-directed reply, and pray that your seed-of-life somehow takes root and begins to grow in that person's heart.

God Gives Us His Spirit Of Love

Love should be the motive behind your behavior. Jeff, love motivated your mom to be a living sacrifice of praise — to courageously represent God's love to your grandparents for over 30 years.

If Jesus is truly your master, then love your neighbor as yourself. However, if money is your master, then greed will drive your behavior and you will manipulate people with counterfeit gifts of love to get what you want. It is a trap! — a pit filled with little masters that rule your behavior.

Greed, power and pleasure bow down to "Master Self." He is the enemy of God's Spirit of love. I have seen a lot of fathers bow down to Master Self on nights and weekends by choosing self-indulging activities over spending quality time with their families. When these activities slip into a Christian husband's or father's lifestyle *on a regular basis*, then the enemy has won.

Instead of giving the gift of time to his child, Master Self *buys and gives* the gift of disappointment — and wraps it with a phony hug, a cheesy smile and empty lips that say, "Look what daddy bought you." Unfortunately, some Christians actually believe that a doll, a bicycle, a video game or a car can take the place of their time, presence and love.

Counterfeit love is the enemy's way of exchanging God's true love for a worthless store-bought gift. Son, please invest in your family (when you have one) and portray God's love — not the love portrayed by philosophers and songwriters who justify their selfish behavior with comments like, "Who cares? — after all, what *is* love?"

Although countless movies, books and songs have been written about love, few agree on what love *is* — but every spouse and every child knows exactly what love *isn't*. Why is love a mystery? After all, hasn't everyone heard the definition of love at almost every wedding?

> Love is patient, love is kind. It does not envy, it does not boast, it is not proud. It does not dishonor others, it is not self-seeking, it is not easily angered, it keeps no record of wrongs. Love does not delight in evil but rejoices with the truth. It always protects, always trusts,

> always hopes, always perseveres. Love never fails (1 Corinthians 13:4-8 NIV).

Son, that *is* love. The real love of our Messiah, not the counterfeit love of the enemy. It is the motive behind the hope of our salvation and it is the emotion we feel when we think of Jesus dying on the cross for us. Therefore, Christians have a duty to demonstrate *this* love — God's love — to their spouses and children, and to every neighbor that God moves close to them.

God Gives Us His Spirit Of Self-Discipline

> For God has not given us a spirit of cowardice, but of power and love and self-discipline (2 Timothy 1:7 LEB).

Jeff, once again, Paul used a word in this verse that is used only once in this exact form in the entire Bible. Most Bibles translate this Greek word as "discipline, self-discipline or control" others as "sober or being sober-minded." When studying the variations of this word and how Peter, Paul and Luke used it, in my opinion, this specific word seems to mean this: *God gives us a powerful Spirit — His mind — to overcome our every natural weakness — to help us see and think clearly — to control our sinful desires, thoughts and temptations — to behave and act like a Christian.*

For God has not given us a spirit of cowardice, but of power, love and the ability to act like a Christian!

Warriors Have Courage

Son, dig into this. Understand what this word means *and* what it does not mean. Otherwise you will fall into the "try harder" trap with its self-help tools and willpower solutions.

For example, in the last chapter, I mentioned that I struggled with situational praise and thanksgiving — that I seemed to thank God only when things turned out great or as I expected. But if I have *God's* Spirit of self-discipline, as I define it, and apply it to "praising God in all situations," then I must simply trust God with every outcome — to release control and know that He loves me and cares for me *and* my family — no matter what!

So put on the powerful armor of God, praise Him, and give up control. Then with faith, hope and love, let God turn your unusual skills, gifts and talents into valuable assets to be a courageous superconqueror who wins — God's way.

Chapter 9

Priests Forgive

Early in my career, I was promoted to Advertising Manager over a few of my more experienced peers in the marketing department. When this happened, one of my colleagues began to treat me with great disrespect. As soon as I became her supervisor, she disagreed with me on every topic. At first I ignored it — figured it was sour grapes. Then I prayed she would get over it, but she didn't.

I could *not* figure her out; she just hated me!

Late one afternoon, I considered ending the war by just firing her. But for some reason, I went into my office, closed the door and prayed, "What happened to her Lord? Why does she hate me so much?"

Then, I calmly invited her into my office to attempt a truce — but she wanted war! She started in again and worked herself into a rage. She yelled so loud that I think they heard her on the golf course outside the building. I actually just sat there and calmly took it while she went on and on and on.

Finally, her 15-minute scream-fest ended with, "And you look just like my ex-husband!"

Bingo! I leaned forward and with a calm voice said, "Jane, I'm not your ex-husband." She stopped and caught her breath. I continued with, "I'm actually a pretty nice guy — a family man with a wonderful wife and great kids." I paused and looked at her with compassion as I softly repeated, "Jane, I'm not your ex-husband."

Her face returned to its normal color and she stood up and started to walk out. Then she turned and said, "You're right, you aren't my ex-husband."

We got along fine after that.

Forgive Those Who Hurt You

> And forgive us our debts, as we also have forgiven our debtors. For if you forgive other people when they sin against you, your heavenly Father will also forgive you. But if you do not forgive others their sins, your Father will not forgive your sins (Matthew 6:12, 14-15 NIV).

Forgiveness is an important and often overlooked aspect of the Lord's Prayer. Jesus teaches us how to pray and how to forgive without discrimination. We are to forgive both intentional and unintentional sins against us. Did you ever look at the Lord's Prayer this way? Essentially God is saying, "It doesn't matter why he or she hurt you, you must forgive ... and then I will forgive you."

Son, as you know, I had a souped-up Chevy when I was in high school. For some strange reason, my loud and speedy muscle car attracted constant attention from policemen who were more than happy to add another ticket to my citation collection.

I finally learned my lesson when I tried to talk my way out of another ticket by claiming ignorance of the law — a law called "excessive noise." Really? You mean that there is actually a law against super loud cars?

When I finished pleading my case, the officer had the nerve to tell me it was my responsibility to know the law. Then he smiled and handed me the ticket. After I calmed down, I knew he was right. It was indeed my responsibility to know the law. So I paid the ticket, fixed my exhaust system and sold the car.

Son, our Jewish ancestors thoroughly knew God's laws and the penalties for breaking them. They longed for a Messiah who would remove their intentional and unintentional law-breaking sins forever — the one who would eliminate the need for regular sacrifices including "The Guilt Offering" as described in this Old Testament passage:

> If anyone sins and does what is forbidden in any of the LORD'S commands, even though they do not know it, they are guilty and will be held responsible. They are to

> bring to the priest as a guilt offering a ram from the flock, one without defect and of the proper value. In this way the priest will make atonement for them for the wrong they have committed unintentionally, and they will be forgiven. It is a guilt offering they have been guilty of wrongdoing against the LORD (Leviticus 5:17-19 NIV).

Jesus our Messiah, died on the cross for *all* of our sins. He was the unblemished sacrifice and substitute Guilt Offering to *permanently* wash away every kind of sin. We were guilty — we broke the law and yet He forgave us as if it never happened.

Do Not Judge

Do not judge, or you too will be judged. For in the same way you judge others, you will be judged, and with the measure *you* use, it will be measured to *you*.

Why do you look at the speck of sawdust in your brother's eye and pay no attention to the plank in your own eye? How can you say to your brother, 'Let me take the speck out of *your* eye,' when all the time there is a plank in your *own* eye?

You hypocrite, first take the plank out of your own eye, and then you will see clearly to remove the speck from your brother's eye (Matthew 7:1-5 NIV, emphasis added).

Jesus commands us to "not judge" or pronounce a guilty sentence on another person. Rather, we are to look at the log in our *own* eyes and consider our *own* issues. This broad command is not narrowly focused on judging *only* your brother's sin. On the contrary, it encompasses our temptation to judge everyone's current "state of affairs." In other words, do not quickly jump to any conclusion as to why someone seems to have hit bottom or appears to be on top of the world. In all cases, it is crystal clear — do not judge!

Forgiveness and judgment become opposing forces when we attempt to be the plaintiff, defendant, lawyer, judge and jury. If we view everyone and every circumstance through this narrow, self-righteous lens, then we will live a life of war. Remember what Jesus said:

> [A]nd with the measure you use, it will be measured to you (Matthew 7:2 NIV).

How do you avoid a life of constant war? — by becoming a peacemaker. Peacemakers do not pick fights. Think about it. If *you* pick fights, and you know that *Satan* picks fights, then won't you always be at war? Here is what the Bible says:

> Blessed are the peacemakers, for they will be called children of God. Blessed are those who are persecuted because of righteousness, for theirs is the kingdom of heaven.

Priests Forgive

> Blessed are you when people insult you, persecute you and falsely say all kinds of evil against you because of me.
>
> Rejoice and be glad, because great is your reward in heaven, for in the same way they persecuted the prophets who were before you (Matthew 5:9-12 NIV).

Unrighteous warriors pick fights and start wars. Son, thankfully, you are a peacemaker and a child of God. But as Jesus points out, being a Christ follower is not all that easy. You *will* be persecuted because of your unwavering Christian values. Jesus does not say *if* you are insulted, persecuted and falsely accused, He says *when*. So when this happens, try to look at the big picture and trust God and allow His Holy Spirit to guide you through it.

Son, I did not get a lot of quality time with my dad when I was growing up; he was always working. Our large family was expensive and dad worked every overtime shift that was offered at one of the nation's largest railroads. He had a job that no one wanted — the demurrage clerk. Essentially, if any railcar was lost or detained, they called dad to solve the problem.

Everyday, he called transportation hubs across the country to get answers. Customers yelled at him over the phone when their expensive cargo was lost or delayed. It must have been stressful. There were no cell phones, GPS tracking devices, central databases, computers or the Internet — just paper records, the

U.S. Postal Service and landline telephones. But dad persevered — day after day, year after year, for decades.

After he retired, we finally talked about a few father/son topics that eluded us during those busy, early years. While eating breakfast at a local restaurant one Saturday morning, I learned that dad was the equivalent of a Gunnery Sergeant in the Merchant Marines during WWII. When he was not conducting training stateside in New York, he played his trombone in the Merchant Marine Marching Band. Why Merchant Marines, you are thinking? My mom said that he was a "4-F" with a bad heart, caused by rheumatic fever he had when he was a kid. He made the best of it and served our country where he could.

On another occasion, dad spoke about his big band days in New York City after the war. He smiled as he talked about making $500/week as a top musician while living in a fancy, Manhattan hotel. Then he kind of dropped a bomb on me. When he finished his breakfast he said, "Son, I'm so proud of you! You're doing just great." Tearing up he continued, "But I've been such a failure. I wanted to provide so many things for your mother and you kids, but I just didn't have the money. I didn't make enough. Please forgive me, I've been such a failure."

I was stunned by dad's transparency. But why was he telling me this? And then it hit me; although it is hard to admit, I was pretty mad at my dad while I was in college. Unlike my rich friends who tapped into their trust funds to pay for college, I did not get any help from my parents or my grandparents.

Jeff, I knew my parents did not have the money, but it didn't matter. I somehow felt entitled to a free ride. Although I never said anything, somehow dad knew it — my body language or general demeanor must have tipped him off.

Anyhow, in hopes of cheering him up, I told him that he was a great provider — that he had sacrificed a lot for all of us. At that point, the conversation became a bit awkward so I cracked a few jokes to ease the tension. Dad chuckled a little and then he changed the subject. We moved away shortly after that and dad died (unexpectedly) a few months later.

As far as I know, "keeping up with the Joneses" is not the 11th commandment. Dad made a responsible decision to leave the music business in 1947 to settle down and raise a family in the Promised Land called California.

Dad gave up a lot. He traded fame and fortune for a loving wife and a big family.

He was a quiet and humble man, a devoted husband and a good provider. He took a job that no one wanted. He did it because he loved us.

Give Up Your Right To Be Right

Son, I know this is a hard teaching. It is difficult to give up your right-to-be-right. The enemy has wedged himself so tightly into the church that it is nearly impossible to force him out. Every day he turns husband against wife, mother against daughter, father against son, brother against sister, boss against employee and pastor against saint. Satan divides marriages by locking the door of reconciliation with the key of unforgiveness.

The only way to break this cycle is to give up your right-to-be-right — to see others through the compassionate eyes of Jesus and to forgive. The Holy Spirit can be trusted to give you what you need, precisely when you need it, so that you can carry out the will of God in your life. So give up your right-to-be-right and forgive.

I experienced a rare type of forgiveness in a business setting many years ago. I am not sure if stupidity is a sin, but I could have been fired for what I said to a reporter. Maybe I should have known better, but my eagerness to please everyone got the best of me when I was a young product manager. It was a great job and I did my best to manage the products and every crisis that surfaced throughout the entire state of California.

After a few months on the job, I was added to a National Product Selection team to pick a new telephone system vendor. We had our eyes on Northern Telecom. Back then, they were one of the top three manufacturers in the world and we had been negotiating with them for more than a year.

I was the youngest member of our national team and completely unaware of Satan's next move.

Priests Forgive

I received a phone call from an experienced reporter one morning. He was fishing for a story and used one of the oldest tricks in the book on me. When the small talk ended, he casually asked, "Hey, how's the Northern Telecom deal going?"

I replied, "Well, not so good — we're kind of stalled right now." And then it got quiet.

A chill came over me when I realized that I had spilled the beans. And to make matters worse I said, "Oh, that comment about Northern — that's off the record — don't write about that." His tone changed as he drilled-down for more. I clammed up and ended the call. I was a goner.

I sat alone in my cubical trying to figure a way out of this mess. A few minutes later, I picked up the phone to brief our product team VP on the East Coast, but it was not really a briefing, it was more like a confession. After he heard the story, he hung up on me.

Then I really started to sweat.

He called me back a few minutes later and said (with a stern formal voice) that he would have to discuss this "breach of confidentiality" with the Chairman of the Board of our $30 billion dollar company.

Then he hung up again.

I told my boss everything, but he just stared at me. So I hid in my cubical, shuffling papers and gazing out the window for the rest of the day.

I did not tell your mom anything when I got home; watering the lawn seemed like a better plan. With hose in hand I prayed, "Lord, I really screwed this thing up. I deserve to get fired. Help me ... Cindi is pregnant and *I need this job*." I pleaded with the Lord to somehow give me a miracle. I actually prayed that the president of our division, who liked me, would think that this whole thing was funny and would give me another chance.

After dinner, I told your mom that I had a bad day, but I still did not share the details. We prayed later that evening, but I did not sleep well that night.

Everyone was quiet the next morning. I felt like a condemned, death row prisoner as I got off the elevator and walked down the long corridor to my cubical.

I caught eyes with a few of my co-workers. I knew that they knew — in fact, it was already all over the company!

At 8:30 a.m., the president showed up at my cubical. He sat down and firmly asked, "How's it going?"

"Well, I've had better days," I replied.

Without blinking he said, "You f*#@*d up."

I looked down and said, "Yep."

And after a few long seconds he said, "Did you learn anything?"

"Yep," I replied. He paused to let it sink in. It seemed like an eternity.

Then he laughed and told me a story of how he also screwed up his first big news interview at a Fortune 500 Company in the early seventies! I was floored.

He got up, smacked me on the back and said loudly, "Good. Well, I guess this thing will speed up the deal — it's about time." Then he swaggered down the long corridor to the elevator and shouted back in my direction, so that everyone could hear, "It's been taking forever to get this deal done. Klena, this should speed it up."

He was right! Our corporate guys signed the deal two days later and sent out a formal press release just ahead of the reporter's story. I was saved, and over the next few years, the president actually promoted me — twice.

Looking back, I am humbled that I learned this important aspect of forgiveness from a powerful executive. His act of forgiveness was an incredible answer to prayer. Son, God moved that day and I will never forget it.

If You Forgive Others, God Will Forgive You

What about acts of malice? You know, the real nasty stuff — getting stabbed in the back or betrayed — words or actions that destroy a career, a friendship or a marriage? Jesus tells us to forgive others … just as He forgives us.

Now let us switch this around with an example where *you* hurt someone.

Although you are saved and are heading to Heaven, when *you* intentionally hurt someone, you increase your debt on God's balance sheet. You create a general ledger posting with the victim's name on it — you owe him! Or as the saying goes, "You owe him an apology."

Your posting sits on the ledger until you hear the Holy Spirit's suggestion to pay the debt with a sincere apology. But if you remain bitter and ignore the debt, your heart gets harder and harder — and the debt grows and grows. So what can you do?

Only the Lord can tell you exactly what to do in each situation — whether you hurt someone or they hurt you. But here is a prediction — you will be the recipient of many injustices throughout your life. When — not if — you are hurt, please stop and remember to forgive — often and every time, as the Bible suggests in this passage:

> Then Peter came to Jesus and asked, "Lord, how many times shall I forgive my brother or sister who sins against me? Up to seven times?" Jesus answered, "I tell you, not seven times, but seventy-seven times" (Matthew 18:21-22 NIV).

Priests Forgive

Your mom and I are amateur counselors and we have not had much success in fixing others' marriages. Years of punishing arguments and unforgiveness are difficult to erase overnight. A clever quote, a Bible verse or an annoying cliché will not heal a broken marriage.

Only the power of God can change an unforgiving heart. Again, *only* the power of God can change an unforgiving heart. So when we are in a counseling situation, we simply pray that God will change a husband or wife's unforgiving heart and that they will finally see each other through the eyes of Jesus.

Son, when it comes to forgiveness, I do not always get it right. Sure, I have resented fellow employees, bosses, close friends and family for one thing or another. But I have not done it for long. The Holy Spirit *always and quickly* convicts me. It is not perfect, but I always get there. I repent fast and give up my right-to-be-right and forgive. The repent-fast habit destroys the enemy's plans as the Holy Spirit refills my heart with peace and joy — while He mends the fabric of every damaged relationship.

Chapter 10

Warriors Play War Games

Son, in the late nineties, you wanted to see a movie about a bug. "Dad, when can we see it?" was all I heard every night at the dinner table.

After some calendar planning, your mom and I hosted a Saturday afternoon getaway that included your little buddy, JD. You probably do not remember this, but back then you were always hungry, so we stopped for a quick lunch at your favorite restaurant before the movie.

A few minutes into our lunch, you whispered something to JD — something funny enough to make you both giggle. We were in a hurry to get to the movie, so I gave you my best *hurry-up* look.

You ignored my look and motioned for me to turn around and take a look at something. Like a secret agent, I dropped my napkin and casually turned around for a casual glance.

Warriors Play War Games

Bam! A nice looking, big-busted woman was sitting right behind me. I was speechless. Then I wondered, "Wait a second, how does my seven-year-old son even know about this kind of stuff?"

You and JD just giggled away so I gave you another look. This time you held out your arms like you were hugging a large barrel and whispered across the table, "Dad, they're huge!"

I was shocked! Well, technically I was only somewhat shocked since I agreed with you. Nevertheless, I gave you my very best KNOCK-IT-OFF look, but you two just continued to giggle. "Do not engage; just ignore him," I told myself. That did not work either.

"Dad, Dad, Daaaaaad," you insisted.

Then with your tongue hanging out and your eyes rolling around, you blasted, "Dad, they're huuuuge!"

Houston, we have a problem.

Somehow your mom was distracted and was not aware of your huge discovery at the restaurant, but with all of your and JD's giggling, she knew something was up.

Son, I cannot remember exactly how I attempted to explain things to her on the way to the theater, but I do recall your mom interrupting my explanation with something like, "What? Where did Jeff learn about that stuff?"

Without any plan, and like most guys under heavy, artillery fire, I just shut down the conversation with, "I'll handle it."

Jeff, thankfully you had polished off a large soda and had to pee pretty bad by the time we arrived at the theater. After we purchased our tickets, I followed you as you dashed into the bathroom.

While side-by-side at the urinals, I calmly asked, "Jeff, at the restaurant..." but you quickly interrupted.

"Dad, did you see that lady? She had the BIGGEST PLATE OF NACHOS I've ever seen! THEY WERE HUGE!"

I thought, "Yep, they were HUGE nachos all right."

Your mom laughed pretty hard when I told her the story — *and that was that.*

Warriors Play War Games

Maybe you are wondering why I included this particular story in a chapter called *War Games*. It is because the story ended well; as I wrote above, *and that was that*. But son, life is full of surprises like the "Nacho Lady," that do not end so well.

Like me in that story, some people react poorly to life's surprises by jumping to conclusions and incorrectly judging situations. So be fully aware of Satan's war games and do not be tricked as the Apostle Paul reminded us:

> [I]n order that Satan might not outwit us. For we are not unaware of his schemes (2 Corinthians 2:11 NIV).

Warriors Play War Games

Paul did not precede this verse with military-like maneuvers as you might expect. On the contrary, Paul preceded this verse by asking church leaders to show mercy and welcome back a penitent brother. His reasons were simple: in order that Satan might not outwit us — For we are not unaware of his schemes — or his mind, as I pointed out in an earlier chapter.

Here are all seven verses in context:

> If anyone has caused grief, he has not so much grieved me as he has grieved all of you to some extent—not to put it too severely. The punishment inflicted on him by the majority is sufficient. Now instead, you ought to forgive and comfort him, so that he will not be overwhelmed by excessive sorrow. I urge you, therefore, to reaffirm your love for him. Another reason I wrote you was to see if you would stand the test and be obedient in everything.
>
> Anyone you forgive, I also forgive. And what I have forgiven — if there was anything to forgive — I have forgiven in the sight of Christ for your sake, in order that Satan might not outwit us. For we are not unaware of his schemes (2 Corinthians 2:5-11 NIV).

Son, war games are hypothetical situations that reveal potential strengths and weaknesses in battle. With that in mind, Satan's war games are designed to divide and conquer — specifically, to divide your relationships and to conquer you. He plays his war games all the time. They are hard to see because he uses a highly effective camouflage called "the element of surprise." But for the grace of God, the Nacho Lady story had a happy ending. Some would call this luck, but I know that without the mind of Christ, that funny story would not have ended with a laugh.

As I have already mentioned, I used to be an angry fighter looking for war. So to make my point, I have created four hypothetical situations, or war games, surrounding the Nacho Lady incident. These scenarios were highly probable if I had reacted with the old mind of Rich Klena, from long ago.

War-game #1: You are the enemy

Jeff, what if I had never asked you for an explanation? What if I never learned the truth? I could have blown you out of the water with a lecture regarding your terrible behavior and punished you with a week of extra chores and confining you to your room! I could have called your Sunday school teacher for his advice on what to do with my son, the pervert.

Do you think this is farfetched? I could have made it even worse if I had called JD's parents and accused them of teaching you inappropriate things. Doesn't this reaction seem reasonable since JD was your giggling accomplice? I could have made a real mess by jumping to conclusions and pronouncing you "guilty" without allowing you an opportunity to explain. Thankfully I did not respond in this way, making you out to be the enemy.

War-game #2: I am the enemy

Your mom and I could have had a serious argument in the car on the way to the movies. She could have jumped to conclusions and attacked me — accusing me of teaching you inappropriate ways of looking at women. Or she could have insinuated something deeper about me with, "So what were YOU actually looking at?"

Do you think I am off my rocker? Hardly. This is how Satan does it. This is how he uses a crazy, surprise situation to sink his evil talons into your mind to split up relationships. But here is the good news, your mom did not react like that at all.

War-game #3: My wife (your mom) is the enemy

I could have lied about the Nacho Lady all together. That would have been easy, since your mom was not entirely aware of the lunch dialogue. Have you ever heard the phrase, "The best defense is a good offense?"

Some husbands use this strategy on their wives all the time. While traveling in the car to the theater, I could have explained the nacho event to her with a slight twist. I could have implied that your mom was to blame for your perversion; that she had not been doing her job and was not watching you close enough. "Did Jeff see any dirty magazines at so-and-so's house?" Followed by, "Cindi, is there anything else that you need to tell me?" Thankfully, I did not lie and attack my wife like she was the enemy.

War-game #4: God is the enemy

In this example, Satan launches a self-righteous missile right at God. I could have said, "Honey, I don't know how Jeffrey got this way. We've done everything right — provided him a good church, the right school, nice friends and a great home. Who did this to him? Where was God when we needed Him? Why didn't He protect him? Clearly, Jeff isn't learning how to behave at our church, so let's look for a new one." Thankfully, I did not react this way and none of this happened.

Son, please do not take this war game exercise the wrong way. Am I bragging that I got this right? Am I being self-righteous? No, on both counts; let me explain.

After five years of marriage, your mom and I started a pattern of snapping at each other. It began with little, sarcastic remarks that smoldered and burned — quirks or petty comments about little things that do not really matter — even minor, personality characteristics that we allowed to bug us.

Then one day we came to our senses. We both recognized this pattern and prayed for a solution. We realized that it was *the small stuff* that was driving a wedge between us! We agreed to cut each other some slack — to ignore the small stuff unless it became a bigger problem or a noticeable pattern. Our "Small Stuff Agreement" was actually a truce that ended potential battles before they could even get started.

Strengthen Relationships With God's Love

> Do you think anyone is going to be able to drive a wedge between us and Christ's love for us? There is no way! Not trouble, not hard times, not hatred, not hunger, not homelessness, not threats, not backstabbing, not even the worst sins listed in Scripture: They kill us in cold blood because they hate you. We're sitting ducks; they pick us off one by one.
>
> None of this fazes us because Jesus loves us. I'm absolutely convinced that nothing—nothing living or dead, angelic or demonic, today or tomorrow, high or low, thinkable or unthinkable—absolutely nothing can get between us and God's love because of the way that Jesus our Master has embraced us (Romans 8:32-35 MSG).

Warriors play war games by recognizing Satan's schemes. Or, as we discovered in Chapter 4, by recognizing Satan's mind. Warriors win war games when they consider the big picture and share the Gospel. Warriors win war games by standing firm in their priest and warrior identities and trusting the love of God — a powerful, everlasting love that nothing can separate.

However, Satan's primary objective is to destroy your faith and hope in God, thus attempting to separate you from His love. Satan never abandons this battlefront nor his ongoing war to destroy all of your relationships.

So what is your strategy? How will you win when Satan tries to destroy the following?

- Your relationship with God
- Your relationship with others
- Your relationship with yourself

Satan Tries To Destroy Your Relationship With God

As you already know, Satan's first area of attack is to separate and destroy your relationship with God. He may start with the same, three temptations he used on Jesus in the desert. He may use a false teaching to instill doubt in the Good News of the Gospel of grace. Or he may fire a few, sneaky weapons right at your weaknesses, to cause you to lose hope. After all, he has been studying you since birth.

But remember, *Satan is not God*. Although he is the master of lies and the ruler of this world, *he is not all knowing and he cannot read your mind*! Although you cannot see him, he sees you. He sees what you do and he hears what you say. Your words have power — power to curse or to bless. Therefore, you must think about how you act and what you say.

I am fairly aware of what I do, but not as aware of what I say. A sarcastic comment or a worldly cliché can chip away at my faith and degrade my behavior. If a few weeks go by without any serious prayer or daily reflection, I degenerate. I can feel it. I know that something has changed for the worse. Somehow, I have allowed Satan to wedge some of his "wrong mind" into my "right mind" through neglect or sin.

Looking back, this mind-creep seems to occur when I am buried at work — endless emails, projects and emergencies crowd out my duty to pray and spend time with the Lord. From my experience, mind-creep is very dangerous because my thoughts slowly change. I do not focus on the Kingdom of God as the enemy camouflages my degrading behavior.

Here is what is frightening — my new behavior seems right — it seems to fit me. Why is this? Well, in my case, this new behavior is actually just my old behavior, or my old mind.

Mind-creep strengthens my ability to succeed by relying on my old wits. When this happens, Satan re-introduces an old friend, Mr. Self-Reliance.

This guy is very capable and he looks marvelous. He proudly marches back into my life and takes over. He knows how to play the game at work and he speaks their language. After a while, he invites my other old friends, Fear and Intimidation to join our old-lifestyle party.

If I do not recognize what is happening, I will happily hang out with these guys. Although my circumstances may improve for a while, and I may feel powerful and in control, I am actually just living like my old self again. I begin to think and live by prideful one-liners like, "You can do anything you want, if you put your mind to it."

Although sayings like this are subtle, they take the place of truth, and reinforce the enemy's lies and mind games. Ultimately, if left unchecked, they will replace your faith and separate you from God!

Son, I am not promoting futility thinking, I am just pointing out how easily weeks can turn into months, and months into years when you neglect your relationship with God. If you find yourself playing this war game — put God first and win!

Satan Tries To Destroy Your Relationship With Others

This is where things get complicated. If you are actively advancing the Kingdom of God, you will attract demonic adversity and get into trouble. When this happens, put on all the armor of God and stand firm against the flaming arrows of the enemy.[18] Bosses play mind games. Friends play mind games. You may even play mind games with yourself.

Life is not simple and it is not all about *one* thing.

The reality is — God is complicated; creation is complicated; people are complicated; Christianity is complicated; and therefore, life is complicated.

If you embrace your identity as a priest and a warrior, allowing the mind of Christ to truly transform your nature into His nature, then you will do the will of God and win.

Following Christ requires faith and courage. It requires instruction, teaching, training and daily guidance from the Holy Spirit. So be on your guard and react with your right mind when you encounter surprises — like the Nacho Lady!

Satan Tries To Destroy Your Relationship With Yourself

Before I met Jesus, I had a love/hate relationship with myself. As I mentioned in Chapter 1, I thought if I fed myself with worldly things, then I would become super happy. It was a lie. I did not feel that way at all. In fact, I felt empty and I hated myself.

Son, have you ever felt this way? I have never asked you this question so I do not really know. But if you have felt this way know that only Jesus can break this love/hate cycle. He breaks it with His love.

I am embarrassed to admit that I have experienced certain aspects of this love/have cycle as a Christian — up and down; happy and unhappy; content and frustrated.

When this happens, the Holy Spirit quickly shows me that the enemy has gained a portion of my mind and filled it with old lies about my identity.

You are a Priest and a Warrior

If these temptations and cycles show up in your life please recognize them for what they are and run to Jesus for help — He is the only answer. He will give you insight into the real problem and help get you back on track. He will remind you that you have been transformed into a different person — a superconqueror who wins!

God loves you and He will always rescue you, even when your head is all screwed up. He has done it for me — He has done it for others — He will do it for you.

Peter's head was pretty messed up after Jesus' death and resurrection. His love/hate relationship with himself was messing him up and steering others off course. I think that Peter just could not forgive himself for denying his relationship with Christ when it mattered the most.

The Bible suggests that at least four of the 12 disciples were very tight with each other — two sets of brothers who were also business partners.[19] These four guys loved Jesus and each other, and they had each other's backs no matter what. But Peter violated this unwritten code of honor. He was not a traitor like Judas — but still he blew it — and everyone knew it.

Today's counselors might say that Peter's recent trauma caused depression. Nevertheless, his "issues" were affecting his family, friends and his Messiah. So, like most men with messed-up heads — he punted! He headed back to his old life — a familiar setting and his old identity in his family's fishing business. This is precisely when Jesus decided to have a breakfast meeting.

Jesus encouraged them all to quickly get back on track — to fulfill their destiny and complete their Great Commission. "Try the other side of the boat," He suggested[20].

> A haul of 153 fish convinced the boys that Jesus still had it — He was still in the miracle business. However, Jesus did not completely have their hearts. That is why this campfire discussion proved to be quite uncomfortable for all of them, especially Peter.
>
> When they had finished eating, Jesus said to Simon Peter, "Simon son of John, do you love me more than these?"
>
> "Yes, Lord," he said, "you know that I love you."
>
> Jesus said, "Feed my lambs."
>
> Again Jesus said, "Simon son of John, do you love me?"
>
> He answered, "Yes, Lord, you know that I love you."
>
> Jesus said, "Take care of my sheep."
>
> The third time he said to him, "Simon son of John, do you love me?"
>
> Peter was hurt because Jesus asked him the third time, "Do you love me?" He said, "Lord, you know all things; you know that I love you."

You are a Priest and a Warrior

Jesus said, "Feed my sheep" (John 21:15-17 NIV).

What is not obvious in this discussion is how Jesus addressed Peter. As you can plainly see, He says, "Simon son of John" (or Simon Johnson), "do you love me more than these?" Sounds kind of formal, doesn't it? After all, didn't everyone just call him Rocky?

Jesus formally asks him if he loves Him more than his friends/relatives. He uses the Greek word *agapao*[21], the verb form of *agape*, which means a deep love, as God loves His children. But Peter replies with "Yes Lord, you know I love you like a brother" (my paraphrase). Interestingly, Peter uses the Greek word *phileo*[22] — commonly known as the type of love between friends or brothers — the same word used in "Philadelphia," the city of brotherly love.

Jesus asks him a second time, "Do you love me?" again using the word *agapao*. Peter again replies, "Yes, I like you," still using *phileo*. The third time Jesus asks, "Simon Johnson, do you like me?" this time switching to the word *phileo*. Peter replies, "You know everything, you know that I like you," using the word for brotherly love in all three of his responses.

It is hard to determine if Peter is confused or if he has an attitude during this exchange. Jesus formally asks Peter to feed His lambs and take care of His sheep — but only if he deeply loves Him. Either Peter does not understand or he does not bite on the offer. So Jesus ends with, if you are my friend (*phileo*) then feed my sheep.

When you read the entire New Testament, including both of the letters Peter wrote to the churches, you will conclude that Peter did indeed "feed His lambs" — the new believers on the Day of Pentecost. Peter also "took care of His sheep" and subsequently "fed His sheep," — the Church, as he fulfilled the Great Commission during his life. Peter ultimately *agapao'd* the Messiah by doing as He asked. Peter was a priest and a warrior — and he finished well.

Chapter 11

Priests Pursue Peace

Shalom is a Hebrew word meaning peace, harmony, fullness, wholeness, completeness, prosperity, welfare and tranquility.[23] However, most people only know it as a Jewish greeting or farewell blessing.

When you read about the peace or shalom of God in the Bible, consider shalom's broader definition, and how it describes your life.

Are you at peace? Are you peacemaker?

As it is written:

> Peacemakers who sow in peace raise a harvest of righteousness (James 3:18 NIV).

I believe that no one can truly experience the peace of God without first making peace with God.

Although you may experience peace (and quiet) when you are alone with a good book and some hot tea, you are not really experiencing the shalom or peace of God that is portrayed in the Bible.

Let us study the connection between God and peace in these three ways:

- Making peace with God
- Experiencing peace from God
- Sharing the peace of God

Making Peace with God

The shalom or peace of God begins with making peace with God, or as some say, surrendering *to* God. I surrendered to God when I was 20 years old. You surrendered to God when you were about 12. But I know a lot of guys that just will not surrender to God. They deny the truth and live an unsettled life as they remain distant or at war with God.

These "no-surrender" people are in every social and demographic category. It does not matter if they are rich or poor, healthy or sick, white or black, Yankee or Rebel, etc.

Thankfully, some come to their senses and accept the truth about the Gospel and finally surrender to God. Others hang on to their pride to the end of their life.

I had an unusual conversation with a brilliant scientist a few years ago. This particular man was an MD/PhD, a surgeon, a renowned researcher and a distinguished expert in his field of medicine. He and I became friends as we worked closely together on some projects for my company.

Like most high-profile scientists, when interviewed, he referenced facts and peer-reviewed research to support his opinions. He was a pro, and he carefully avoided publicly acknowledging any existence of God. But in private, and with his permission, we often discussed various topics that, in my opinion, provided evidence of God and His Creation.

While we were eating lunch together one day, I casually asked him, "Doc, how does the human ear actually work?"

Jeff, I hit a nerve! He put down his fork and replied with animated frustration, "We don't really know! Rich, the more we learn, the less we know. We can tell you what it *does*, but we haven't the slightest idea of *how* it does it. In fact, we don't actually know how the body does anything!"

I was stunned with his humble and honest response. We had a few more discussions like this, but he never actually acknowledged the existence of the Almighty Creator — the great I Am.

While driving home after those discussions, I often prayed that Doc would someday recognize the limits of his genius mind and surrender to the God that has all the answers — the God who created everything.

Some highly intelligent people resist God and live without answers and without peace. They worship their own IQ, but their frustration turns to cynicism when they cannot figure everything out. To compensate, they invent answers or theories about the origin of life and pawn these off as "facts."

Son, when you hear the word "theorize" brace yourself, because you are about to encounter a wild speculation (which often requires far more faith than believing in God). If only these brilliant intellectuals would realize that God created the very mind that they are using to theorize on life's questions.

Experiencing Peace from God

Just after Jesus' resurrection, he appeared to the fearful disciples who were hiding in the Upper Room behind locked doors. Suddenly He appeared and greeted them with *Shalom aleikhem*[24] (Hebrew: עֲלֵיכֶם שָׁלוֹם) with means "peace be upon you.[25]"

Then He showed them the proof of His resurrection:

> Having greeted them, he showed them his hands and his side. The talmidim were overjoyed to see the Lord. "Shalom aleikhem!" Yeshua repeated. "Just as the Father sent me, I myself am also sending you."

> Having said this, he breathed on them and said to them, "Receive the Ruach HaKodesh! If you forgive someone's sins, their sins are forgiven; if you hold them, they are held" (John 20:20-23 CJB).

You are a Priest and a Warrior

Son, after He greeted them, He breathed His Holy Spirit into their discouraged hearts. Likewise, we receive His Holy Spirit when we surrender and make our peace with Him. Then, we experience His peace and are ready to become peacemakers.

Making, experiencing and sharing peace begins with intentionality. Jesus said:

> Blessed are the peacemakers, for they shall be called sons of God (Matthew 5:9 NASB).

If you are not intentional about pursuing peace, then you will end up with war. Son, it is one or the other. But here is the good news, David and Peter may have been "men of war" in their youth, but over time, they both pursued peace and had "many good days" as it is written by David in Psalms and then quoted by Peter in his first epistle:

> Whoever of you loves life and desires to see many good days, keep your tongue from evil and your lips from speaking lies. Turn from evil and do good; seek peace and pursue it (Psalm 34:12-14 NIV).

> "Whoever would love life, and see good days must keep his tongue from evil and his lips from deceitful speech. He must turn from evil and do good; he must seek peace and pursue it" (1 Peter 3:10-11 NIV).

As we learned in earlier chapters, Satan uses all of his weapons to wage war against God and you. He places difficult relationships and challenging situations in your path to steal your peace and rob your joy.

Today's smartphones are fantastic; they provide ways to find instant answers to almost any question. They also help friends stay connected by providing a platform to share details of their lives with each other. Although they are a blessing, constant distractions and carefully timed interruptions by the enemy are now commonplace with every user — including Christians.

Worry, fear and hopelessness are continually pushed into our lives via social media and news headlines. Without rules or boundaries, dealing with constant anxiety will become the "new norm" as Satan slowly separates us from God's peace.

Son, stop and think about this. Ask God to help you recognize these peace-stealing interruptions, then be intentional about seeking peace and pursuing it.

When you are alone with God in prayer or meditation, turn off the world! Separate yourself *for* God. Make a decision to *be* a peacemaker and experience the peace (or the complete shalom) of God — and then share it with someone.

Sharing the Peace of God

It is easy to have peace and to share it during the good seasons of your life, but what about the hard seasons — like when you find yourself in the middle of a hairy, family battle? That is when tempers fly and arguments soar!

You are a Priest and a Warrior

Inspired by God, the Book of James is filled with more than 50 direct commands on how to win God's way as a priest and a warrior. He did not mess around with long stories, or tiptoe his way through subjects. James challenged the church with straight talk on everything — especially on how to avoid war and make peace by controlling one's own tongue — the only thing in Creation that cannot be tamed.

Consider if this straight talk from James applies to you.

> Likewise the tongue is a small part of the body, but it makes great boasts. Consider what a great forest is set on fire by a small spark. The tongue also is a fire, a world of evil among the parts of the body. It corrupts the whole person, sets the whole course of his life on fire, and is itself set on fire by hell.
>
> All kinds of animals, birds, reptiles and creatures of the sea are being tamed and have been tamed by man, but no man can tame the tongue. It is a restless evil — full of deadly poison.
>
> With the tongue we praise our Lord and Father, and with it we curse men, who have been made in God's likeness. Out of the same mouth come praise and cursing. My brothers, this should not be (James 3:5-10 NIV).

Priests Pursue Peace

Son, just as you cannot put toothpaste back in the tube, you cannot put mean and hurtful words back in your mouth.

Unfortunately, many relationships, marriages and business partnerships have been destroyed with careless, fighting words. A big, fat mouth is a *dangerous* weapon.

This is precisely why the Bible is filled with warnings regarding the power of the tongue. Solomon wrote:

> The tongue has the power of life and death, and those who love it will eat its fruit (Proverbs 18:21 NIV).

James continues with:

> Who is wise and understanding among you? Let him show it by his good life, by deeds done — in the humility that comes from wisdom" (James 3:13 NIV).

Then he explains true wisdom — what it looks like, when it is used, and how pure wisdom from Heaven produces peace:

> Who is wise and understanding among you? Let him show it by his good life, by deeds done in the humility that comes from wisdom.
>
> But if you harbor bitter envy and selfish ambition in your hearts, do not boast about it or deny the truth. Such "wisdom" does not come down from heaven but is earthly, unspiritual, of the devil. For where you have envy and selfish ambition, there you find disorder and every evil practice.

> But the wisdom that comes from heaven is first of all pure; then peace-loving, considerate, submissive, full of mercy and good fruit, impartial and sincere. Peacemakers who sow in peace raise a harvest of righteousness (James 3:13-18 NIV).

Jeff, what is a harvest of righteousness? Is it the "fruit of the Spirit?" Well, not exactly. A harvest of righteousness is the fruit that comes from the testimony of one's life! It is the testimony of our marriage, our family, our children, our employees, our coworkers and our friends — it is our behavior in every situation that glorifies God as He waters His seed of eternal life in us with His peaceful love and tender mercy.

Pursue A Peaceful Marriage

Son, once in a while, I am asked about my marriage or the secret to a happy marriage. When this happens, I normally throw out a cliché like, "Well, you have to be intentional about it, so invest in it," or "be nice to your wife," and then I usually shift the discussion to something else. After all, how can anyone summarize decades of decisions over a cup of coffee?

In marriage, every day has its challenges, conflicts and ample opportunities to pick a fight. As I mentioned in the last chapter, it usually starts with the small stuff — a snide comment, a stare or giving your spouse the silent treatment.

Priests Pursue Peace

These insidious, little sparks light fires that burn out of control. Early on, I realized that my marriage did not have a chance without God. I knew that we would not make it without our collective resolve to share peace with each other.

If you want something tangible to think about, here is my simple marriage formula: 1+1+1= 1, or Rich + Cindi + Jesus = One Good Marriage. It may seem corny, but that is our reality.

Son, you and Jesus together are already *one*, so keep this marriage formula in mind as you search for a godly woman — one who also is like-minded with Christ — and therefore can be like-minded with you.

There is nothing like a peaceful marriage. It is worth pursuing. And if you get it, you will experience a bit of Heaven on Earth.

Shalom

Chapter 12

Warriors Have Faith

> Guard, through the Holy Spirit who dwells in us, the treasure which has been entrusted to you (2 Timothy 1:14 NASB).

When I was a junior in college, I worked nights and weekends as a part-time manager for a grocery store chain in Southern California. The television commercials often ended with a cameo shot of a store manager wearing a blue sport coat saying, "Tell a friend." My mom loved those commercials and the snazzy blue coats! She even came into the grocery store one evening to snap a picture of me — her "Man in Blue."

I found that photograph tucked away in a shoebox after my mom passed away. It brought back some good memories — and one really bad one — from a Sunday night in 1981.

At 9:55 p.m., I said goodbye to the last customer and walked over to Sherri, our cashier, to help her close down her cash register for the evening. Just then, a man wearing a mask ran up to me, the "Man in Blue," and announced his hostile intentions by shoving a gun in my back. I cleaned out Sherri's cash register for him and stood there hoping he would leave. Instead he pushed the gun harder into my back and demanded, "The safe."

Now I had a problem.

There were actually three safes in one large housing, stacked on top of each other. The safe in the middle held the weekend's big money. It was a time-lock safe and I had already set it to *only* open after 6:00 a.m. the next morning — our company policy. I tried to explain this situation to the robber — why I was unable to open it for him — but he did not care. He knew the big haul was in that box so he shouted over and over, "Open it!"

To try and appease him, I gave him my wallet and cleaned out the small bills and coin rolls from the top and bottom safes. It was not enough; he continued to shout and point at the middle safe while I continued to insist it could not be opened. It was a bad situation. With the gun to my back, he then pushed me outside the grocery store.

I heard voices from a car hidden around the corner yelling to their accomplice behind me, "We gotta go!"

I stopped in my tracks and pleaded with him, "Dude, I didn't see anything — nothing — just go."

Again they yelled, "Come on!" I stayed frozen where I was standing.

He paused for a second and then pointed the gun between my eyes. "Turn around and don't look back, or I'll pop you in the head," he threatened.

With my eyes shut and my hands behind my head, I slowly turned around.

For the next few moments, I felt like a blindfolded prisoner in front of a firing squad — cringing and waiting for *the shot*. Instead, I finally heard the sound of screeching tires as the thieves peeled out of the parking lot.

Sherri, crying and hysterical, ran over and hugged me as I wobbled back into the store. After I collected myself, I called the police and the store manager. When I described the robbery to the police officers, they said that we were both lucky to be alive.

When the store manager arrived, the first thing out of my mouth was an apology for having lost the company's money — thinking I was supposed to guard it with my life. With compassion, the old manager replied that no amount of money was worth Sherri and my lives.

Your Faith Is Your Treasure

Son, your faith is your treasure. It is everything you believe about what you should believe. Let me say that again, your faith is everything you believe about what you *should* believe. As I said in Chapter 1, your priest and warrior identity is your lifetime constant. When you became a Christian, God separated you from the rest of the dead and lifeless rocks on the side of the road — to be His living stone — carefully placed in His spiritual house, to be part of His holy priesthood.

> You also, like living stones, are being built into a spiritual house to be a holy priesthood, offering spiritual sacrifices acceptable to God through Jesus Christ (1 Peter 2:5 NIV).

Jesus is your trustworthy cornerstone. Build your life on Him. When the enemy attacks you use your "mind of Christ" to expose his tricks that steer you away from the Gospel of Jesus Christ. Consider this:

> For we are not struggling against human beings, but against the rulers, authorities and cosmic powers governing this darkness, against the spiritual forces of evil in the heavenly realm (Ephesians 6:12 CJB).

Satan and his evil army have bombarded the church with false teachings for thousands of years. Paul challenged the early church to stick to *"the gospel I preached to you."*

> Now, brothers and sisters, I want to remind you of the gospel I preached to you, which you received and on which you have taken your stand. By this gospel you are saved, if you hold firmly to the word I preached to you. Otherwise, you have believed in vain. For what I received I passed on to you as of first importance: that

> Christ died for our sins according to the Scriptures, that he was buried, that he was raised on the third day according to the Scriptures, and that he appeared to Cephas, and then to the Twelve. After that, he appeared to more than five hundred of the brothers and sisters at the same time, most of whom are still living, though some have fallen asleep. Then he appeared to James, then to all the apostles, and last of all he appeared to me also … (1 Corinthians 15:1-8 NIV).

Son, your faith is supported with facts. Yes, I said *facts*, not theories or blind faith. Based on the sheer volume of eyewitness testimonies of the risen Jesus, any reasonable and prudent person would conclude that the resurrection actually happened. Therefore, if the resurrection happened, then Jesus was not just another prophet or teacher. He proved that He is the Messiah and the Son of God.

This is the Good News — *this* is the Gospel you believe — *this* is your faith and your treasure.

Guard Your Treasure

> Guard, through the Holy Spirit who dwells in us, the treasure which has been entrusted to you (2 Timothy 1:14 NASB).

Jeff, the Holy Spirit has lived inside of you for many years. He is your friend, counselor and guiding light. But, "It's a long life"

Warriors Have Faith

and you cannot guard your faith your entire life without a powerful union with God.

As you read in Chapter 5, the power in priests comes from the Holy Spirit and God's powerful armor and spiritual weapons. Each piece of armor, like the sword of the Spirit, provides protection from the constant attacks of the enemy. God's armor is at your disposal — to be used by you — a superconqueror.

Guard your treasure through the power of the Holy Spirit, who:

- Flows into you and makes you a holy priest and a mighty warrior
- Flows out of you with power and love
- Gives you supernatural courage to share the Good News
- Allows you to hear His crystal clear voice inside of you
- Spurs you to take action
- Enables you to speak truth in love to a wavering, Christian brother
- Enables you to forgive liars, cheaters and those who hurt you
- Heals the sick and feeds the poor
- Helps you love your neighbor as yourself
- Extinguishes all of the fiery arrows of the enemy

- Gives you the shalom of God to enjoy life

He is the gift, the deposit, the prize and the treasure that you must protect — a portion of your great inheritance that is waiting for you.

> Praise be to the God and Father of our Lord Jesus Christ! In his great mercy he has given us new birth into a living hope through the resurrection of Jesus Christ from the dead, and into an inheritance that can never perish, spoil or fade. This inheritance is kept in heaven for you (1 Peter 1:3-4 NIV).

Jeff, your inheritance in Heaven is your living hope and your ultimate treasure. However, you live in the "now and the not yet." This is why God has not left you all alone as an orphan. His Holy Spirit lives inside of you to guide and comfort you. He is your helmet of salvation, your sword of protection, and your bridge from the now to the not yet of eternal life in Heaven.

* * *

Heavenly Father,

I praise you and I thank You for my son Jeff. He honors me and he honors You with the testimony of his life. Hear this prayer, Lord, and protect him by the power of Your Holy Spirit. Let him grow in his faith — a faith that has been revealed to him by your Son Jesus. Help him to guard his treasure, every day, through the Holy Spirit.

Warriors Have Faith

Let him serve in Your house as a holy priest — offering his life as spiritual sacrifice acceptable to You. Help him to grow as a superconqueror through Your Son, Jesus Christ. Give him insight into Your Kingdom and show him the enemy's destructive plans in advance, so that he may stand his ground.

Show him Your power in his weakness and remind him to put on Your armor every day. Help him prepare his mind for action and to be intentional about his purpose and representation of You as a son in Your chosen family. And remind him to praise You in all situations — good or bad — as we do not know Your plans.

Lord, give him the courage and the confidence to live a righteous life that is empowered by Your Holy Spirit. Help him see others as You see them so that he may be able to forgive them as You forgive him.

Pour out Your grace on him, and give him insight into whom he is fighting, seeing the accuser for what he is — a liar, who comes to rob, kill and destroy.

Jeff has a mature and solid faith in You, and the hope of salvation through Your Son Jesus. Honor his faith and guard his treasure with Your holy Word, Your powerful sword of the Spirit, to testify to Your glory. Show him my love and Your love. Show him how to live out his freedom in You and to enjoy Your way of life that gives liberty, freedom, joy and shalom.

In Jesus' name,

Amen.

Notes and References

[1] Owen, John. *Pneumatologia, Or, A Discourse concerning the Holy Spirit Wherein an Account Is given of His Name, Nature, Personality, Dispensation, Operations, and Effects : His Whole Work in the Old and New Creation Is Explained, the Doctrine Concerning It Vindicated F*. Printed by F. Darby, for Nathaniel Ponder ..., 1657, reprint 2nd ed. Vol. 1. London. 1808. *P 402*. Print.

[2] Matthew 28:18.

[3] Zacharias, Ravi K. *Jesus among Other Gods: The Absolute Claims of the Christian Message*. Nashville, TN: Word Pub., 2000. *Climbing a Massive Wall; Pp 6,7*. Print. Jesus Among Other Gods by Ravi Zacharias © 2000 Ravi Zacharias. *And is used by permission* of Thomas Nelson. www.thomasnelson.com.

[4] Chambers, Oswald . Taken from *My Utmost for His Highest* by Oswald Chambers, © l935 by Dodd Mead & Co., renewed © 1963 by the Oswald Chambers Publications Assn., Ltd., *and is used by permission* of Discovery House, Box 3566, Grand Rapids MI 4950l. All rights reserved. *"August 15th entry."*

[5] 2 Peter 3:11.

[6] Strong, James, and James Strong. *The New Strong's Exhaustive Concordance of the Bible: With Main Concordance, Appendix to the Main Concordance, Key Verse Comparison Chart, Dictionary of the Hebrew Bible, Dictionary of the Greek Testament*. Nashville: Thomas Nelson, 1984. Print.

[7] Lewis, C.S. Taken from *MERE CHRISTIANITY* by CS © copyright CS Lewis Pte Ltd 1942, 1943, 1944, 1952. *And is used by permission* from The CS Lewis Company Ltd, 1st Floor Unit 4 Old Generator House, Bourne Valley Road, Poole BH12 1DZ UK. Chapter: *What Christians Believe, pp 53, 54*.

[8] Young, Robert. *Young's Analytical Concordance to the Bible: Containing*

Notes and References

About 311,000 References Subdivided Under the Hebrew and Greek Originals with the Literal Meaning and Pronunciation of Each : Based Upon the King James Version. , 1982. Print.
Strong, James, and James Strong. *The New Strong's Exhaustive Concordance of the Bible: With Main Concordance, Appendix to the Main Concordance, Key Verse Comparison Chart, Dictionary of the Hebrew Bible, Dictionary of the Greek Testament.* Nashville: Thomas Nelson, 1984. Print.

9 Young, Robert. *Young's Analytical Concordance to the Bible: Containing About 311,000 References Subdivided Under the Hebrew and Greek Originals with the Literal Meaning and Pronunciation of Each : Based Upon the King James Version. , 1982. Print.*
Strong, James, and James Strong. *The New Strong's Exhaustive Concordance of the Bible: With Main Concordance, Appendix to the Main Concordance, Key Verse Comparison Chart, Dictionary of the Hebrew Bible, Dictionary of the Greek Testament.* Nashville: Thomas Nelson, 1984. Print.

10 What you are Fighting: *The enemy the Worldcontroller is also known as:* Satan (Luke 10:18); The Serpent (Gen. 3:4); The Accuser (Rev. 12:10); The Adversary (1 Pet. 5:8, KJV); A Murderer/Father of lies (John 8:44); Angel of the abyss (Rev. 9:11); Prince of demons (Matt. 12:24); The Ruler of the powers of the air (Eph. 2:2); The Prince of this world (John. 14:30); God of this world (2 Cor. 4:4); Wicked One (Matt. 13:19, KJV). *The Enemy manipulates our minds to:* Instigate evil (John 13:2,27); Tempt man to sin (Gen. 3:17). Undo God's work (Mark 4:15); Secure men's worship (Luke 4:6-8; 2 Thes. 2:3,4); Make men turn away from God (Job 2:4,5); *The Enemy is an evil father to his children:* They do his will (John 8:44); He blinds them (2 Cor. 4:4); He deceives them (Rev 20:7-8); He troubles them (1 Sam. 16:14); They will all perish with him (Matt. 25:41). *Although we are God's children, Satan has the power to:* Tempt us (1 Chr. 21:1); Attack our health (Job 2:7); Accuse us (Zech. 3:1); Sift us (Luke 22:31); Lead us astray (2 Cor. 11:3); Seize our property (Job 1:13-17);

Believe his lying teachers (2 Cor. 11:13-15); To devour us (1 Pet 5:8). *But as Christians we are to:* Be aware of his schemes so that he doesn't trick us (2 Cor. 2:11); Fight against him (Eph. 6:11-16); Resist him (James 4:7, 1 Pet 5:9); Overcome him (1 John 2:13, Rev. 12:10-11).

[11] "John Owen." *John Owen*. Web Accessed. 17 July 2014. <http://www.johnowen.org/>. *Timeline of Owen's Life*.

[12] Owen, John. *Pneumatologia, Or, A Discourse concerning the Holy Spirit Wherein an Account Is given of His Name, Nature, Personality, Dispensation, Operations, and Effects : His Whole Work in the Old and New Creation Is Explained, the Doctrine Concerning It Vindicated F*. Printed by F. Darby, for Nathaniel Ponder ..., 1657, reprint 2nd ed. Vol. 1. London. 1808. *Pp 392,394,395*. Print.

[13] "Voyage of the St. Louis." *United States Holocaust Memorial Museum*. United States Holocaust Memorial Council, 20 June 2014. Web Accessed. 27 Oct. 2014. <http://www.ushmm.org/wlc/en/article.php? Module Id=10005267>

[14] Barker, Kenneth L., and Donald W. Burdick. *The NIV Study Bible, New International Version*. Grand Rapids, Mich., U.S.A.: Zondervan Bible, 1985. *Study notes Psalm 145, note section, p 145*. Print.

[15] LORD (Dt. 6:4; Dan. 9:14); The Lord Will Provide (Ge. 22:14); The Lord Who Heals (Ex. 15:26); The Lord Our Banner (Ex. 17:15); The Lord Who Sanctifies and Makes Us Holy (Lev. 20:8; Ez. 37:28); The Lord Our Peace (Jdg. 6:24); LORD God (Ge. 2:4; Ps. 59:5); The Lord Our Righteousness (Jer. 33:16); Everlasting God (Ge. 21:33; Ps. 90:1-3); The Mighty One of Jacob (Ge. 49:24; Ps. 132:2, 5); Ancient of Days (Dan. 7:9, 13, 22); Our Creator (Isa. 40:28, 43:15); Our Deliverer (2 Sam. 22:2; Ps. 18:2, 40:17, 70:5); Our Advocate (Job 16:19, 1 John 2:1); Holy One (Isa. 43:15); I AM (Ex. 3:14); Judge (Ps. 75:7); King (Ps. 10:16, 47:2, 98:6, 149:2); Lawgiver (Isa. 33:22); Light (Ps. 27:1); Most High (2 Sam. 22:14; Ps. 9:2, 73:11, 107:11); Rock (1 Sam 2:2); Rock of

Notes and References

Israel (2 Sam 23:3); Rock of My Refuge (Ps 94:22); Rock of My Salvation (2 Sam 22:47); Redeemer (Isa 54:8); Shepherd of Israel (Ps 80:1); Father (Isa. 64:8); Papa (Mk. 14:36; Ro. 8:15; Gal. 4:6) The First and Last/Alpha and Omega (Rev. 1:8, 22:13).

[16] 1 Samuel 17:36.

[17] Dohrenwend, PhD., Robert E. The Sling, Forgotten firepower of antiquity, Journal of Asian Martial Arts, volume 11 number 2 – 2002, p 40. Used with permission from www.viamediapublishing.com.

[18] Ephesians 6:16.

[19] Luke 5:1-10.

[20] John 21:6.

[21] Young, Robert. *Young's Analytical Concordance to the Bible: Containing About 311,000 References Subdivided Under the Hebrew and Greek Originals with the Literal Meaning and Pronunciation of Each : Based Upon the King James Version. , 1982. Print.* " agapao."

[22] Young, Robert. *Young's Analytical Concordance to the Bible: Containing About 311,000 References Subdivided Under the Hebrew and Greek Originals with the Literal Meaning and Pronunciation of Each : Based Upon the King James Version. , 1982. Print.* "phileo."

[23] "Shalom." Wikipedia. Wikimedia Foundation. 16 Sept. 2014. *And* Stern, David H. *Jewish New Testament Commentary: A Companion Volume to the Jewish New Testament.* Clarksville, Md.: Jewish New Testament Publications, 1992. Print. *(Explanation of the word, Shalom).* And Strong, James, and James Strong. *The New Strong's Exhaustive Concordance of the Bible: With Main Concordance, Appendix to the Main Concordance, Key Verse Comparison Chart, Dictionary of the Hebrew Bible, Dictionary of the Greek Testament.* Nashville: Thomas Nelson, 1984. Print.

[24] "Shalom Aleikhem." Wikipedia. Wikimedia Foundation. 16 Sept. 2014.

Stern, David H. *Jewish New Testament Commentary: A Companion Volume to the Jewish New Testament*. Clarksville, Md.: Jewish New Testament Publications, 1992. Print. Strong, James, and James Strong. *The New Strong's Exhaustive Concordance of the Bible: With Main Concordance, Appendix to the Main Concordance, Key Verse Comparison Chart, Dictionary of the Hebrew Bible, Dictionary of the Greek Testament*. Nashville: Thomas Nelson, 1984. Print.

[25] John 20:19.

Made in the USA
Lexington, KY
17 September 2017